CompTIA A+®
2006 Q&A

Chimborazo, LLC

THOMSON

™

COURSE TECHNOLOGY

Professional ■ Technical ■ Reference

Important: Thomson Course Technology PTR cannot provide software support. Please contact the appropriate software manufacturer's technical support line or Web site for assistance.

Thomson Course Technology PTR and the author have attempted throughout this book to distinguish proprietary trademarks from descriptive terms by following the capitalization style used by the manufacturer.

Information contained in this book has been obtained by Thomson Course Technology PTR from sources believed to be reliable. However, because of the possibility of human or mechanical error by our sources, Thomson Course Technology PTR, or others, the Publisher does not guarantee the accuracy, adequacy, or completeness of any information and is not responsible for any errors or omissions or the results obtained from use of such information. Readers should be particularly aware of the fact that the Internet is an ever-changing entity. Some facts may have changed since this book went to press.

Educational facilities, companies, and organizations interested in multiple copies or licensing of this book should contact the Publisher for quantity discount information. Training manuals, CD-ROMs, and portions of this book are also available individually or can be tailored for specific needs.

ISBN-10: 1-59863-352-X

ISBN-13: 978-1-59863-352-8

Library of Congress Catalog Card Number: 2006908263

Printed in Canada

07 08 09 10 11 PH 10 9 8 7 6 5 4 3

Publisher and General Manager, Thomson Course Technology PTR:
Stacy L. Hiquet

Associate Director of Marketing:
Sarah O'Donnell

Manager of Editorial Services:
Heather Talbot

Marketing Manager:
Mark Hughes

Acquisitions Editor:
Megan Belanger

Marketing Assistant:
Adena Flitt

Project Editor/Proofreader:
Karen A. Gill

Technical Reviewers:
Susan Whalen, Serge Palladino

PTR Editorial Services Coordinator:
Erin Johnson

Interior Layout Tech:
Bill Hartman

Cover Designer:
Mike Tanamachi

Indexer:
Kevin Broccoli

THOMSON

COURSE TECHNOLOGY ™

Professional ■ Technical ■ Reference

Thomson Course Technology PTR, a division of Thomson Learning Inc.
25 Thomson Place ■ Boston, MA 02210 ■ http://www.courseptr.com

CONTENTS

1

COMPTIA A+ ESSENTIALS

QUESTION 1

What is the primary input device of a computer?

A. Printer

B. Monitor

C. Keyboard

D. CPU

EXPLANATION

The keyboard is the primary input device of a computer.

QUESTION 2

What is the name of a pointing device used to move a pointer on the screen and to make selections?

A. Keyboard

B. Printer

C. Monitor

D. Mouse

EXPLANATION

A mouse is a pointing device used to move a pointer on the screen and to make selections.

QUESTION 3

What is the name of the visual device that displays the primary output of the computer?

A. Monitor

B. Mouse

C. Keyboard

D. Modem

EXPLANATION

The monitor is the visual device that displays the primary output of the computer.

QUESTION 4

What is the name of the device that produces output on paper, often called hard copy?
A. Keyboard
B. Mouse
C. Monitor
D. Printer

EXPLANATION

A very important output device is the printer, which produces output on paper, often called hard copy.

QUESTION 5

What other type of printer is popular today besides ink-jet, laser, solid ink, and dot-matrix?
A. Ergonomic
B. Optic
C. Thermal
D. Sound

EXPLANATION

The most popular printers available today are ink-jet, laser, thermal, solid ink, and dot-matrix.

QUESTION 6

What technology is most often used to manufacture microchips?
A. BIOS
B. TTL
C. CMOS
D. TTY

EXPLANATION

All circuit boards contain microchips, which are most often manufactured using complementary metal-oxide semiconductor (CMOS) technology.

QUESTION 7

What is the name of a device that is not installed directly on the motherboard?
A. Integrated circuit
B. Microchip
C. Embedded circuit
D. Peripheral device

EXPLANATION

A device that is not installed directly on the motherboard is called a peripheral device.

QUESTION 8

What is the name of the port that connects to an external home theater audio system, providing digital output and the best signal quality?

A. Serial port

B. USB port

C. S/PDIF port

D. Parallel port

EXPLANATION

An S/PDIF (Sony-Philips Digital Interface) sound port connects to an external home theater audio system, providing digital output and the best signal quality.

QUESTION 9

What is the name of the port provided by some older motherboards that transmits data serially?

A. Parallel port

B. Serial port

C. S/PDIF port

D. LAN antenna port

EXPLANATION

Some older motherboards provide a serial port that transmits data serially (one bit follows the next); it is often used for an external modem or a serial mouse (a mouse that uses a serial port).

QUESTION 10

What is the name of the temporary storage that the processor uses to temporarily hold both data and instructions while it is processing them?

A. Secondary storage

B. Memory

C. CMOS

D. BIOS

EXPLANATION

The processor uses temporary storage, called primary storage or memory, to temporarily hold both data and instructions while it is processing them.

QUESTION 11

What is the name of the devices that provide primary storage?
  A. RAM
  B. ROM
  C. CMOS
  D. BIOS

EXPLANATION

Primary storage is provided by devices called memory or random access memory (RAM), located on the motherboard and on other circuit boards.

QUESTION 12

How can you define a sealed case containing platters or disks that rotate at a high speed?
  A. Hard drive
  B. RAM
  C. Volatile drive
  D. ROM

EXPLANATION

A hard drive is a sealed case containing platters or disks that rotate at a high speed.

QUESTION 13

Which type of connector on a motherboard can support one or two EIDE devices?
  A. Serial ATA
  B. RIMM
  C. SIMM
  D. Parallel ATA

EXPLANATION

A parallel ATA connector on a motherboard can support one or two EIDE devices.

QUESTION 14

What is the internal technology that most hard drives use today?
  A. DIMM
  B. IDE
  C. CMOS
  D. SIMM

EXPLANATION

Most hard drives today use an internal technology called Integrated Drive Electronics (IDE).

1

QUESTION 15

Which standard allows for more than four drives installed in a system and applies only to hard drives, not to other drives?

  A. EIDE

  B. Parallel ATA

  C. Serial ATA

  D. IDE

EXPLANATION

The serial ATA standard allows for more than four drives installed in a system and applies only to hard drives, not to other drives.

QUESTION 16

Which secondary storage device is sometimes found inside the case and can hold 3.5-inch disks containing up to 1.44 MB of data?

  A. Zip drive

  B. Floppy drive

  C. CD-ROM drive

  D. DVD drive

EXPLANATION

Another secondary storage device sometimes found inside the case is a floppy drive that can hold 3.5-inch disks containing up to 1.44 MB of data.

QUESTION 17

What is the name for the system of pathways used for communication and the protocol and methods used for transmission?

  A. Power traces

  B. Traces

  C. Bus

  D. Data lines

EXPLANATION

The system of pathways used for communication and the protocol and methods used for transmission are collectively called the bus.

QUESTION 18

What is the name for the lines of the bus used for data?
- A. Power trace
- B. Traces
- C. Protocol bus
- D. Data bus

EXPLANATION

The parts of the bus that we are most familiar with are the lines of the bus that are used for data, called the data bus.

QUESTION 19

What is the width of a data bus called?
- A. Host bus
- B. FSB size
- C. Data path size
- D. System bus size

EXPLANATION

The width of a data bus is called the data path size.

QUESTION 20

What is the name of the component dedicated to timing the activities of the chips on the motherboard?
- A. Host bus
- B. System bus
- C. Front side bus
- D. System clock

EXPLANATION

One of the most interesting lines, or circuits, on a bus is the system clock or system timer, which is dedicated to timing the activities of the chips on the motherboard.

QUESTION 21

Which unit is used to measure the system clock speed?
- A. Bytes
- B. Hertz
- C. Bits
- D. Micron

1

EXPLANATION

The beats, called the clock speed, are measured in hertz (Hz), which is one cycle per second; megahertz (MHz), which is one million cycles per second; and gigahertz (GHz), which is one billion cycles per second.

QUESTION 22

Which expansion slot is used for a video card?

A. AGP
B. ATA
C. ISA
D. IDE

EXPLANATION

A motherboard will have one slot intended for use by a video card. The older board uses an AGP slot for that purpose, and the newer board uses a long PCI Express x16 slot for video.

QUESTION 23

What is the name of the card that provides a port for the monitor?

A. Sound card
B. Network card
C. Video card
D. Modem card

EXPLANATION

The video card provides a port for the monitor.

QUESTION 24

What is the most important component of the computer's electrical system?

A. Power cord
B. Power supply
C. Power bus
D. Host bus

EXPLANATION

The most important component of the computer's electrical system is the power supply, which is usually near the rear of the case.

QUESTION 25

What is the name of the data and instructions used to start the computer that are stored on special ROM chips on the board?

A. BIOS
B. CMOS
C. DIMM
D. SIMM

EXPLANATION

Some basic instructions are stored on the motherboard—just enough to start the computer. These data and instructions are stored on special ROM (read-only memory) chips on the board and are called the BIOS (basic input/output system).

QUESTION 26

The following term is often used to refer to software embedded into hardware:

A. BIOS
B. CMOS
C. Chipset
D. Firmware

EXPLANATION

Software that is embedded into hardware is often referred to as firmware because of its hybrid nature.

QUESTION 27

The following operating system offered several improvements over Windows NT, including a more stable environment:

A. Windows 95
B. Windows 98
C. Windows Me
D. Windows 2000

EXPLANATION

Windows 2000 offered several improvements over Windows NT, including a more stable environment, support for Plug and Play, and features specifically targeting notebook computers.

1

QUESTION 28

You can check the following site to see if your hardware and applications qualify for all Windows 2000 operating systems:

A. testedproducts.windowsmarketplace.com
B. www.testyourproduct.org
C. yourproduct.windows2000.com
D. windows2000.com.yourproducts

EXPLANATION

To see if your hardware and applications qualify, check the Windows Marketplace Tested Products List at testedproducts.windowsmarketplace.com.

QUESTION 29

The following operating system is an upgrade of Windows 2000 and attempts to integrate Windows 9x/Me and 2000:

A. Windows for Groups
B. Windows 3.1
C. Windows NT
D. Windows XP

EXPLANATION

Windows XP is an upgrade of Windows 2000 and attempts to integrate Windows 9x/Me and 2000, while providing added support for multimedia and networking technologies.

QUESTION 30

What is the name of the OS created by Linus Torvalds?

A. Unix
B. Linux
C. MAC OS X
D. Windows 2003

EXPLANATION

A variation of Unix that has recently gained popularity is Linux, an OS created by Linus Torvalds when he was a student at the University of Helsinki in Finland.

QUESTION 31

Windows-style shells for Unix and Linux are sometimes called:
  A. Distribution
  B. Linux source
  C. X Windows
  D. X core

EXPLANATION

Because many users prefer a Windows-style desktop, several applications have been written to provide a GUI shell for Unix and Linux. These shells are called X Windows.

QUESTION 32

The following version of Mac OS offers easy access to the Internet and allows any Macintosh computer to become a Web server for a small network:
  A. Mac OS 5i
  B. Mac OS 6.5
  C. Mac OS 9i
  D. Mac OS X

EXPLANATION

Mac OS X offers easy access to the Internet and allows any Macintosh computer to become a Web server for a small network.

QUESTION 33

The following term means you can boot a computer into one of two installed OSs:
  A. Dual boot
  B. BIOS
  C. CMOS
  D. RIMM

EXPLANATION

A dual boot makes it possible to boot a computer into one of two installed OSs.

QUESTION 34

What is the name of the program that functions as the GUI for the Mac OS?
  A. Toolbar
  B. Finder
  C. Dock
  D. X Windows

EXPLANATION

When a Mac is turned on, a program called the Finder is automatically launched. This is the program that provides the desktop.

QUESTION 35

Which of the following is an OS main function?

A. Managing files
B. Turning the computer on
C. Checking power supply problems
D. Checking data bus problems

EXPLANATION

All OSs share the following four main functions: providing a user interface, managing files, managing applications, and managing hardware.

QUESTION 36

What is the name of an OS internal component that relates to users and applications?

A. Kernel
B. Registry
C. File system
D. Shell

EXPLANATION

A shell is the portion of the OS that relates to the user and to applications.

QUESTION 37

What is the name of the OS internal component that interacts with the computer hardware?

A. Shell
B. Kernel
C. Control Panel
D. Registry

EXPLANATION

The core, or kernel, of the OS is responsible for interacting with hardware.

QUESTION 38

What is the name of the Windows database for hardware and software configuration information?

A. Kernel
B. Control Panel
C. Registry
D. Shell

EXPLANATION

Windows uses a database called the registry for most of this hardware and software configuration information.

QUESTION 39

Windows text files with .ini or .inf extensions are called:

A. Registry files
B. Initialization files
C. Shell files
D. Kernel files

EXPLANATION

Windows keeps some hardware and software data in text files called initialization files, which often have an .ini or .inf file extension.

QUESTION 40

The following type of interface allows you to type commands to tell the OS what to do:

A. Command-driven interface
B. Menu-driven interface
C. Mouse-driven interface
D. Icon-driven interface

EXPLANATION

With a command-driven interface, you type commands to tell the OS to perform operations.

QUESTION 41

The following command arranges data on your hard drive for better performance:

A. Run
B. Star
C. Defrag
D. Find

EXPLANATION

Defrag is the command to arrange data on your hard drive for better performance.

QUESTION 42

The following type of interface allows you to perform operations by clicking on small pictures on the screen:
  A. Prompt-driven interface
  B. Menu-driven interface
  C. Command-driven interface
  D. Icon-driven interface

EXPLANATION

With an icon-driven interface, sometimes called a graphical user interface (GUI), you perform operations by clicking icons (or pictures) on the screen.

QUESTION 43

What is the name of the initial screen that appears when an OS is first executed?
  A. Desktop
  B. Command prompt
  C. Icon window
  D. Menu prompt

EXPLANATION

When an OS is first executed, the initial screen that appears, together with its menus, commands, and icons, is called the desktop.

QUESTION 44

An operating system stores files and folders using an organizational method called:
  A. Sector
  B. Tracks
  C. Clusters
  D. File system

EXPLANATION

An operating system is responsible for storing files and folders on a secondary storage device using an organizational method called the file system.

QUESTION 45

For hard drives, Windows uses the following file systems:
  A. FAT and Ext3
  B. FAT and NTFS
  C. Ext2 and Ext3
  D. JFS and Ext3

EXPLANATION

For hard drives, Windows uses either the FAT or the NTFS file system.

QUESTION 46

What is the name of the table of a hard drive that tracks how space on a disk is used to store files?
  A. Tracks
  B. Sectors
  C. File allocation table
  D. Clusters

EXPLANATION

The file allocation table (FAT) is a table on a hard drive or floppy disk that tracks how space on a disk is used to store files.

QUESTION 47

What is the latest version of FAT?
  A. FAT8
  B. FAT16
  C. FAT24
  D. FAT32

EXPLANATION

The latest version of FAT, FAT32, is a more efficient method of organization for large hard drives than FAT16 (the earlier version).

QUESTION 48

The following term describes concentric circles (one circle inside the next) on the disk surface:
  A. Cluster
  B. Tracks
  C. Sector
  D. Maps

EXPLANATION

A hard drive or floppy disk is composed of tracks, which are concentric circles (one circle inside the next) on the disk surface.

QUESTION 49

Each track on a disk contains various segments called:

A. Clusters
B. Sectors
C. Maps
D. Bytes

EXPLANATION

Each track is divided into several segments, each called a sector.

QUESTION 50

What is the smallest unit of space on a disk for storing a file?

A. Cluster
B. Sector
C. Byte
D. Track

EXPLANATION

A cluster, the smallest unit of space on a disk for storing a file, is made up of one or more sectors.

QUESTION 51

What is the name of the first directory table created when a logical drive is formatted?

A. Init directory
B. Main directory
C. Root directory
D. Start directory

EXPLANATION

When each logical drive is formatted, a single directory table is placed on the drive called the root directory.

QUESTION 52

The following term refers to a drive and directories that are pointing to the location of a file:

  A. Path
  B. Folder
  C. Subdirectory
  D. Directory table

EXPLANATION

When you refer to a drive and directories that are pointing to the location of a file, as in C:\wp\data\myfile.txt, the drive and directories are called the path to the file.

QUESTION 53

In a typical filename such as myfile.txt, the portion to the left of the period is called:

  A. File extension
  B. Filename
  C. File type
  D. File ID

EXPLANATION

When naming a file, the first part of the name before the period is called the filename.

QUESTION 54

What part of a filename identifies the file type?

  A. File ID
  B. Filename
  C. Period
  D. File extension

EXPLANATION

The file extension identifies the file type, such as .doc for Microsoft Word document files or .xls for Microsoft Excel spreadsheet files.

QUESTION 55

By clicking Start, Run and entering Diskmgmt.msc in the Run dialog box, you can open the following tool in Windows XP/2000:

  A. Disk Management
  B. Control Panel
  C. Command Prompt
  D. Registry

EXPLANATION

To open the Disk Management utility, click Start, Run and enter Diskmgmt.msc in the Run dialog box. Then press Enter.

QUESTION 56

What is the command used in Windows 9x/Me to create partitions?
A. Defrag
B. Disk Management
C. Fdisk
D. Format

EXPLANATION

For Windows 9x/Me, the Fdisk command is used to create partitions.

QUESTION 57

The following term refers to software that is designed to perform a task for the user:
A. Firmware
B. BIOS
C. ROMware
D. Application

EXPLANATION

Software that is designed to perform a task for the user is called an application.

QUESTION 58

Applications depend on the following to perform background tasks:
A. BIOS
B. Operating system
C. Firmware
D. Bus

EXPLANATION

An application depends on an OS to provide access to hardware resources, to manage its data in memory and in secondary storage, and to perform many other background tasks.

QUESTION 59

In the following mode, the CPU processes 16 bits of data at one time:
A. Extended mode
B. Real mode
C. Protected mode
D. Long mode

EXPLANATION

In 16-bit mode, or real mode, the CPU processes 16 bits of data at one time.

QUESTION 60

In the following mode, the CPU processes 32 bits of data at one time:
A. Real mode
B. Long mode
C. Protected mode
D. Extended mode

EXPLANATION

In 32-bit mode, or protected mode, the CPU processes 32 bits of data at a time.

QUESTION 61

In the following mode, the CPU processes 64 bits of data at one time:
A. Protected mode
B. Extended mode
C. Real mode
D. Long mode

EXPLANATION

In 64-bit mode, or long mode, the CPU processes 64 bits of data at a time.

QUESTION 62

The following operating mode gives applications complete access to hardware resources:
A. Real mode
B. Open mode
C. Basic mode
D. Long mode

EXPLANATION

In real mode, an application has complete access to all hardware resources.

QUESTION 63

The following term means more than one program is working at the same time:
A. Thread
B. Serial computing
C. Cluster tasking
D. Multitasking

EXPLANATION

Multitasking is when more than one program is working at the same time.

QUESTION 64

Which was the first version of Windows to provide preemptive multitasking?
A. Windows 3.1
B. Windows 95
C. Windows 2000
D. Windows XP

EXPLANATION

Windows 95 was the first version of Windows to provide preemptive multitasking.

QUESTION 65

Which was the first version of Windows to support multiprocessing?
A. Windows NT
B. Windows 98
C. Windows XP
D. Windows 2003 Server

EXPLANATION

Windows NT was the first Windows OS to support multiprocessing.

QUESTION 66

Windows 9x/Me and Windows NT/2000/XP all support the following operating mode:
A. Extended mode
B. 8-bit mode
C. 32-bit mode
D. 64-bit mode

EXPLANATION

DOS uses 16-bit mode; Windows 9x/Me and Windows NT/2000/XP all use 32-bit mode, although each OS is backward compatible with earlier modes.

QUESTION 67

All Pentium processors operate in the following mode:
  A. 8-bit mode
  B. 16-bit mode
  C. 32-bit mode
  D. 64-bit mode

EXPLANATION

All Pentium processors operate in 32-bit mode.

QUESTION 68

Software written for Windows 3.x is called:
  A. 8-bit program
  B. 16-bit Windows software
  C. Long mode program
  D. Protected Windows software

EXPLANATION

Software written for Windows 3.x is called 16-bit Windows software.

QUESTION 69

Software programs written for Windows NT/2000/XP and Windows 9x/Me are called:
  A. 8-bit Windows software
  B. 16-bit programs
  C. Real mode programs
  D. 32-bit programs

EXPLANATION

Software programs written for Windows NT/2000/XP and Windows 9x/Me are called 32-bit programs.

QUESTION 70

The operating system uses which of the following components to relate to the hardware?
  A. Device drivers and BIOS
  B. CMOS and TTL
  C. Firmware and TTL
  D. CMOS and BIOS

1

EXPLANATION

An operating system is responsible for communicating with hardware, but the OS does not relate directly to the hardware. Rather, the OS uses device drivers or the BIOS to do the job.

QUESTION 71

What is the term used to refer to small programs stored on the hard drive that tell the computer how to communicate with a specific hardware device?

A. BIOS

B. CMOS

C. Device drivers

D. TTL

EXPLANATION

Device drivers are small programs stored on the hard drive that tell the computer how to communicate with a specific hardware device

QUESTION 72

Windows Me, Windows NT/2000, Windows XP Home Edition, and Windows XP Professional use only the following type of drivers:

A. 32-bit drivers

B. 64-bit drivers

C. Long-mode drivers

D. Real-mode drivers

EXPLANATION

Windows Me, Windows NT/2000, Windows XP Home Edition, and Windows XP Professional use only 32-bit drivers.

QUESTION 73

Where do Windows 2000/XP and Windows 9x/Me record information about a driver when installing it?

A. Initialization file

B. Disk partition

C. Device partition

D. Windows registry

EXPLANATION

When 32-bit device drivers are installed, Windows 2000/XP and Windows 9x/Me record information about the drivers in the Windows registry.

QUESTION 74

The following is a text file used to configure DOS and Windows 3.x:
  A. Winreg.ini
  B. Config.sys
  C. OS.ini
  D. Bios.sys

EXPLANATION

Config.sys, Autoexec.bat, and System.ini files are text files used to configure DOS and Windows 3.x that Windows 95 and Windows 98 support for backward compatibility.

QUESTION 75

The OS can communicate with simple devices, such as floppy drives or keyboards, using the following:
  A. BIOS
  B. TTL
  C. CMOS
  D. ROM

EXPLANATION

The OS can communicate with simple devices, such as floppy drives or keyboards, through the system BIOS.

QUESTION 76

Which statement is correct regarding device management?
  A. The BIOS is faster than device drivers
  B. Device drivers are faster than the BIOS
  C. Device drivers are slower than the BIOS
  D. The BIOS and device drivers work at the same speed

EXPLANATION

Because device drivers are faster, the trend today is to use device drivers rather than the BIOS to manage devices.

QUESTION 77

What component is responsible for moving data and instructions in and out of memory?
  A. BIOS
  B. Firmware
  C. CMOS
  D. Operating system

1

EXPLANATION

The Operating System (OS) is responsible for moving data and instructions in and out of memory and for keeping up with what is stored where.

QUESTION 78

The following term refers to the method of using the hard drive as though it were RAM:
- A. Real-mode memory
- B. Cache memory
- C. Virtual memory
- D. Page memory

EXPLANATION

The method of using the hard drive as though it were RAM is called virtual memory.

QUESTION 79

Data stored in virtual memory is stored in a file called:
- A. Cache file
- B. RAM file
- C. RIMM file
- D. Swap file

EXPLANATION

Data stored in virtual memory is stored in a file on the hard drive called a swap file or page file.

QUESTION 80

What is the primary tool provided by the Windows shell?
- A. Control Panel
- B. Windows desktop
- C. Windows Explorer
- D. Taskbar

EXPLANATION

The Windows desktop is the primary tool provided by the Windows shell.

QUESTION 81

The following tool allows you to change the way the desktop looks:
   A. Windows Explorer
   B. Taskbar
   C. Display Properties window
   D. Menubar

EXPLANATION

One tool useful for changing the way the desktop looks is the Display Properties window.

QUESTION 82

The following item displays information about open programs and provides quick access to others:
   A. Taskbar
   B. Control Panel
   C. Desktop
   D. Display Properties window

EXPLANATION

The taskbar is normally located at the bottom of the Windows desktop, displaying information about open programs and providing quick access to others.

QUESTION 83

The following term describes a program that runs in the background to support or serve Windows or an application:
   A. Swap
   B. Service
   C. Virtual application
   D. Virtual task

EXPLANATION

A service is a program that runs in the background to support or serve Windows or an application.

1

QUESTION 84

The following item displays icons for running services in Windows XP:

A. System tray
B. Control Panel
C. Windows Explorer
D. Menubar

EXPLANATION

The system tray is on the right side of the taskbar and displays icons for running services; these services include the volume control and network connectivity.

QUESTION 85

In Windows XP, you can create a folder using the following command from a command prompt:

A. CD
B. FDISK
C. MKDIR
D. DIR

EXPLANATION

In Windows XP, you can also create a folder using the MD or MKDIR command from a command prompt.

QUESTION 86

In Windows XP, you can delete a folder using the following command from a command prompt:

A. MKDIR -D
B. MD
C. CD
D. RD

EXPLANATION

In Windows XP, you can also delete a folder using the RD or RMDIR command from a command prompt.

QUESTION 87

In Windows XP, you can change file or folder attributes using the following command from a command prompt:

A. Change

B. Dir

C. Attrib

D. File

EXPLANATION

In Windows XP, you can change the attributes of a file or folder using the Attrib command from a command prompt.

QUESTION 88

The following file attribute indicates that a file belongs to the OS:

A. Hide attribute

B. System attribute

C. Read-only attribute

D. Archive attribute

EXPLANATION

There is one other attribute of a file, called the system attribute, that says a file belongs to the OS.

QUESTION 89

The following term defines a window containing several small utility programs called applets that are used to manage hardware, software, users, and the system.

A. Taskbar

B. Shortcut menu

C. System Properties

D. Control Panel

EXPLANATION

The Control Panel is a window containing several small utility programs called applets that are used to manage hardware, software, users, and the system.

QUESTION 90

The following is an essential tool for PC troubleshooting and maintenance:

A. Ground bracelet
B. Cans of compressed air
C. Cleaning solutions
D. Needle-nose pliers

EXPLANATION

Essential tools for PC troubleshooting include ground bracelet, ground mat, or ground gloves to use when working inside the computer case

QUESTION 91

The following tool is used to pick up a screw that has fallen into a place where hands and fingers can't reach:

A. Torx screwdriver
B. Needle-nose pliers
C. Flat-head screwdriver
D. Extractor

EXPLANATION

When you push down on the top of an extractor, three wire prongs come out that can be used to pick up a screw that has fallen into a place where hands and fingers can't reach.

QUESTION 92

The following tool is used to check the power supply output:

A. Needle-nose pliers
B. Multimeter
C. Flashlight
D. AC outlet ground tester

EXPLANATION

A multimeter can be used to check the power supply output.

QUESTION 93

The following tool can be used to remove jumpers and to hold objects in place while you screw them in:
   A. Needle-nose pliers
   B. Torx screwdriver
   C. Extractor
   D. Chip extractor

EXPLANATION

Needle-nose pliers can be used to remove jumpers and to hold objects in place while you screw them in (especially those pesky nuts on cable connectors).

QUESTION 94

When maintaining or troubleshooting a PC, you should store unused parts in:
   A. Plastic bags
   B. Paper cups
   C. Antistatic bags
   D. Plastic cups

EXPLANATION

Antistatic bags are a type of Farady Cage to store unused parts.

QUESTION 95

The following is used to clean the contacts on expansion cards:
   A. Head cleaner
   B. Contact cleaner
   C. Monitor wipes
   D. Optifix

EXPLANATION

Contact cleaner is used to clean the contacts on expansion cards, which might solve a problem with a faulty connection.

QUESTION 96

The following item includes information such as physical data, toxicity, health effects, first aid, storage, shipping, disposal, and spill procedures for a chemical substance:
   A. Chemical cleaner
   B. Chemical sheet
   C. MSDS
   D. Cleaner sheet

1

EXPLANATION

An MSDS includes information such as physical data, toxicity, health effects, first aid, storage, shipping, disposal, and spill procedures.

QUESTION 97

The following tool can be of great help to discover and report computer errors and conflicts at POST:

    A. POST diagnostic card

    B. LED expansion card

    C. Extractor

    D. Chip diagnostic card

EXPLANATION

Although not an essential tool, a POST diagnostic card can be of great help to discover and report computer errors and conflicts at POST.

QUESTION 98

The following type of plan can help prevent failures and reduce repair costs and downtime:

    A. Disaster recovery plan

    B. PC failure plan

    C. Network failure plan

    D. Preventive maintenance plan

EXPLANATION

If you are responsible for the PCs in an organization, make and implement a preventive maintenance plan to help prevent failures and reduce repair costs and downtime.

QUESTION 99

The following is one of the items that you always need to back up from your computer:

    A. Installed applications

    B. Visited Web pages

    C. E-mail address list

    D. Pirated software

EXPLANATION

You need to keep good backups of data, including your data files, e-mail address list, and e-mail attachments.

QUESTION 100

When you first set up a computer, you need to start the following to help with future maintenance and troubleshooting:

A. Recovery CD
B. Recovery DVD
C. Setup CD
D. Record book

EXPLANATION

When you first set up a new computer, start a record book about this computer, using either a file on disk or a notebook that is dedicated to this machine.

QUESTION 101

What is the tool that prevents hackers or malicious software from getting into your computer without your knowledge?

A. Antivirus software
B. Firewall
C. Recovery CD
D. Antispyware software

EXPLANATION

A firewall is hardware or software that prevents hackers or malicious software from getting into your computer without your knowledge.

QUESTION 102

The following can damage your computer:

A. Tar from cigarettes
B. Keyboard cover
C. Disabling the ability to write to the boot sector of the hard drive
D. Keeping private data encrypted

EXPLANATION

Tar from cigarettes can accumulate on fans, causing them to jam and the system to overheat.

QUESTION 103

How often should you make sure air vents on a PC are clear?

A. Monthly
B. Yearly
C. Every two years
D. Once every five years

1

EXPLANATION

Make sure air vents are clear once a year.

QUESTION 104

How often should you perform backups on your system?
A. Two times a year
B. Yearly
C. Monthly
D. At least weekly

EXPLANATION

You should perform regular backups at least weekly.

QUESTION 105

How often should you clean printers from dust and bits of paper?
A. At least monthly
B. Every six months
C. Yearly
D. Every two years

EXPLANATION

You should clean printers from dust and bits of paper, using compressed air and a vacuum, at least monthly or as recommended by the manufacturer.

QUESTION 106

How often should you check that only authorized software is present on a computer?
A. Monthly
B. Every two months
C. Yearly
D. Every two years

EXPLANATION

If directed by your employer, check that only authorized software is present on a computer at least once a month.

QUESTION 107

The following is a general guideline when preparing to ship a computer:
A. Keep the humidity level high inside the box
B. Keep the temperature level high inside the box
C. Back up the hard drive
D. Keep the temperature level very low inside the box

EXPLANATION

When shipping a computer, back up the hard drive onto a tape cartridge or other backup medium separate from your computer.

QUESTION 108

The following is true when shipping a computer:
  A. Ship a notebook with the power turned on
  B. Remove any removable disks from the drives
  C. Keep humidity level high
  D. Keep the computer in a warm environment before shipping it

EXPLANATION

When preparing to ship a computer, remove any removable disks, tape cartridges, or CDs from the drives.

QUESTION 109

The following is true when shipping a notebook computer:
  A. Remove the battery
  B. Ship the computer with the power turned on
  C. Keep all removable disks in the drives
  D. Keep all power cords connected to the computer

EXPLANATION

Disconnect power cords from the electrical outlet and the devices. Disconnect all external devices from the computer. For notebook computers, remove the battery.

QUESTION 110

Consider purchasing the following when shipping a computer:
  A. A box that barley fits the computer
  B. A box that is twice as big as the computer
  C. A box that is four times as big as the computer
  D. Postal insurance

EXPLANATION

Purchase insurance on the shipment. Postal insurance is not expensive and can save you a lot of money if materials are damaged in transit.

QUESTION 111

You should dispose of alkaline batteries in the following way:

A. Dispose of them in the regular trash
B. Burn them
C. Bury them
D. Smash them

EXPLANATION

Dispose of these batteries in the regular trash. First check to see if there are recycling facilities in your area.

QUESTION 112

You should dispose of button batteries in the following way:

A. Dispose of them in the regular trash
B. Return them to the original dealer
C. Burn them
D. Bury them

EXPLANATION

These batteries can contain silver oxide, mercury, lithium, or cadmium and are considered hazardous waste. Dispose of them by returning them to the original dealer or by taking them to a recycling center.

QUESTION 113

The following is true when working inside a computer case:

A. Stack boards on top of each other
B. Always use a magnetized screwdriver
C. Use a graphite pencil to change DIP switch settings
D. Don't stack boards on top of each other

EXPLANATION

Don't stack boards on top of each other. You could accidentally dislodge a chip this way.

QUESTION 114

The following is true when working inside a computer case:

A. Always touch chips with a magnetized screwdriver
B. Stack boards on top of each other
C. Don't use a graphite pencil to change DIP switch settings
D. Always touch the inside of a computer that is turned on

EXPLANATION

Don't use a graphite pencil to change DIP (dual inline package) switch settings, because graphite is a conductor of electricity, and the graphite can lodge in the switch.

QUESTION 115

Select from the options one of the two types of damage in an electronic component caused by ESD:

A. Ground failure
B. Bracelet failure
C. Dissipate failure
D. Upset failure

EXPLANATION

ESD can cause two types of damage in an electronic component: catastrophic failure and upset failure.

QUESTION 116

The following type of damage caused by ESD destroys the component beyond use:

A. Catastrophic failure
B. Upset failure
C. Bracelet failure
D. Dissipate failure

EXPLANATION

A catastrophic failure destroys the component beyond use.

QUESTION 117

The following type of damage caused by ESD damages the component so that it does not perform well all the time:

A. Bracelet failure
B. Dissipate failure
C. Upset failure
D. Catastrophic failure

EXPLANATION

An upset failure damages the component so that it does not perform well, even though it may still function to some degree.

1

QUESTION 118

A ground bracelet is also called:
  A. Ground mat
  B. ESD bracelet
  C. Catastrophic bracelet
  D. Upset bracelet

EXPLANATION

A ground bracelet, also called an antistatic strap or ESD bracelet, is a strap you wear around your wrist.

QUESTION 119

The following tools dissipate ESD and are commonly used by bench technicians:
  A. Magnetic screwdrivers
  B. Network cable tester
  C. AC outlet ground tester
  D. Ground mats

EXPLANATION

Ground mats dissipate ESD and are commonly used by bench technicians.

QUESTION 120

The following is true when working inside a PC monitor:
  A. You must be grounded
  B. You don't want to be grounded
  C. You must always use ground bracelets
  D. You must always use ESD bracelets

EXPLANATION

You don't want to be grounded when working inside a monitor.

QUESTION 121

The following is true when working inside older AT cases:
  A. You don't want to be grounded
  B. They maintain high electrical charges
  C. Leaving the power cord plugged in helps to ground the case
  D. Catastrophic failures are more likely than upset failures

EXPLANATION

When working inside the older AT cases, it was safe enough to leave the power cord plugged into the power outlet if the power switch was turned off. Leaving the power cord plugged in helped to ground the case.

QUESTION 122

The following is true when working with ATX and BTX cases:
  A. Residual power is still on even when the power is turned off
  B. You don't want to be grounded
  C. Catastrophic failures are more likely than upset failures
  D. Leaving the power cord plugged in helps to ground the case

EXPLANATION

With newer ATX and BTX cases, residual power is still on even when the power switch on the rear of the case is turned off.

QUESTION 123

The following is an essential tool when taking apart a computer:
  A. Magnetic screwdrivers
  B. Network cable tester
  C. Phillips-head screwdriver
  D. POST diagnostic card

EXPLANATION

In most situations, the essential tools you'll need for the job are a ground bracelet, a Phillips-head screwdriver, a flat-head screwdriver, paper, and pen.

QUESTION 124

The following is true when taking apart a computer:
  A. Put the computer on a table with plenty of room
  B. Don't power down the system
  C. You don't need to back up important data on the hard drive
  D. You always need to restore CMOS to its original state

EXPLANATION

Put the computer on a table with plenty of room. Have a plastic bag or cup handy to hold screws.

1

QUESTION 125

The following is true when opening a computer case:

A. All types of case panels have screws on the rear
B. Some case panels don't use screws
C. All types of case panels have screws on the front
D. All types of case panels have screws on one side

EXPLANATION

Know that some case panels don't use screws; these side panels simply pop up and out with a little prying and pulling.

QUESTION 126

The following is true when working on a tower case:

A. Lay it on its bottom so the motherboard is on the left
B. Lay it on its bottom so the motherboard is on the right
C. Lay it on its side so the motherboard is on the top
D. Lay it on its side so the motherboard is on the bottom

EXPLANATION

If you're working on a tower case, lay it on its side so the motherboard is on the bottom.

QUESTION 127

Drives are connected to the motherboard using one of the following options:

A. Serial ATA cables
B. Power cords
C. Grounded cables
D. UTP cables

EXPLANATION

Drives are connected to the motherboard with ribbon cables or thinner serial ATA cables.

QUESTION 128

On a ribbon cable, a red color edge marks that side of the cable as the following:

A. Power pin
B. Ground pin
C. Pin 0
D. Pin 1

EXPLANATION

Before removing any ribbon cables, look for a red color or stripe down one side of each cable. This edge color marks this side of the cable as pin 1.

QUESTION 129

The following is true about notched ribbon cables:
  A. Mark pin 1 with a red color
  B. Mark pin 34 with a red color
  C. Can be inserted in only one direction
  D. Can be inserted in both directions

EXPLANATION

Some boards and drives don't mark the pins, but rather have a notch in the connector so that a notched ribbon cable can only be inserted in one direction.

QUESTION 130

The following is true about Serial ATA cables:
  A. Mark pin 1 using a blue color
  B. Can be connected in only one direction
  C. Mark pin 1 using a red color
  D. Mark pin 1 and pin 40 using a blue color

EXPLANATION

Serial ATA cables can only connect to serial ATA connectors in one direction.

QUESTION 131

How many pins does an IDE ribbon cable have?
  A. 10
  B. 16
  C. 32
  D. 40

EXPLANATION

IDE cables have 40 pins.

1

QUESTION 132

What type of IDE cable do most hard drives use today?

  A. 40-conductor
  B. 80-conductor
  C. 120-conductor
  D. 200-conductor

EXPLANATION

Most hard drives today use the higher quality 80-conductor IDE cable.

QUESTION 133

The following is true about the Molex connector:

  A. It can be connected in only one direction
  B. Marks pin 34 with a red color
  C. Marks pin 40 with a blue color
  D. Molex connector is a type of notched cable

EXPLANATION

Notice as you disconnect the power cord, the Molex connector is shaped so it only connects in one direction.

QUESTION 134

What are the most expensive and most easily damaged parts of a computer system?

  A. Power supply and monitor
  B. Keyboard and mouse
  C. Motherboard and processor
  D. Motherboard and power supply

EXPLANATION

The motherboard and processor are the most expensive and most easily damaged parts in the system.

QUESTION 135

How many main power lines do older AT power supplies and motherboards use?

  A. Only one
  B. Two
  C. Three
  D. Five

EXPLANATION

Older AT power supplies and motherboards use two main power lines that plug in side-by-side on the motherboard and are labeled P8 and P9.

QUESTION 136

The following term refers to the computer bringing itself up to a working state without the user having to do anything but press the on button:

A. BIOS
B. Dual-boot
C. CMOS
D. Booting

EXPLANATION

The term booting comes from the phrase "lifting yourself up by your bootstraps" and refers to the computer bringing itself up to a working state without the user having to do anything but press the on button.

QUESTION 137

The following term involves turning on the computer power with the on/off switch:

A. Hot boot
B. Soft boot
C. Hard boot
D. Software boot

EXPLANATION

A hard boot, or cold boot, involves turning on the power with the on/off switch.

QUESTION 138

The following term involves using the operating system to reboot the computer:

A. Warm boot
B. Cold boot
C. Hard boot
D. Hardware boot

EXPLANATION

A soft boot, or warm boot, involves using the operating system to reboot.

QUESTION 139

Pressing the following keys performs a soft boot in DOS:

A. Ctrl+Alt+Esc
B. Alt+Esc
C. Shift+Alt+Esc
D. Ctrl+Alt+Del

EXPLANATION

For DOS, pressing the keys Ctrl, Alt, and Del (or Delete) at the same time performs a soft boot. (You will often see this key combination written as Ctrl+Alt+Del.)

QUESTION 140

The following is true about booting a computer:

A. A warm boot is more stressful than a soft boot
B. A warm boot is more stressful than a hard boot
C. A hard boot is more stressful than a soft boot
D. A soft boot is more stressful than a cold boot

EXPLANATION

A hard boot is more stressful on your machine than a soft boot because of the initial power surge through the equipment that occurs when you press the power switch.

QUESTION 141

The following is true about booting a computer:

A. A soft boot is faster than a hard boot
B. A cold boot is faster than a hard boot
C. A cold boot is faster than a warm boot
D. A warm boot is faster than a soft boot

EXPLANATION

A soft boot is faster because the initial steps of a hard boot don't happen.

QUESTION 142

The following term defines program code contained on the firmware chip on the motherboard that is responsible for getting a system up and going and finding an OS to load:

A. CMOS boot
B. Startup BIOS
C. LILO boot
D. Startup CMOS

EXPLANATION

The startup BIOS is program code contained on the firmware chip on the motherboard that is responsible for getting a system up and going and finding an OS to load.

QUESTION 143

What is the name of the test performed by the startup BIOS to determine if it can communicate correctly with essential hardware components?
   A. Startup CMOS test
   B. CMOS test
   C. Power-on self test
   D. DIPS test

EXPLANATION

The POST (power-on self test) is a series of tests performed by the startup BIOS to determine if it can communicate correctly with essential hardware components required for a successful boot.

QUESTION 144

The startup BIOS begins the startup process by reading configuration information stored primarily in the following:
   A. PCI slots
   B. CMOS RAM
   C. CMOS PROM
   D. BIOS RAM

EXPLANATION

The startup BIOS begins the startup process by reading configuration information stored primarily in CMOS RAM.

QUESTION 145

The following component searches for and loads an OS:
   A. CMOS RAM
   B. PCI slots
   C. BIOS ROM
   D. Startup BIOS program

EXPLANATION

The startup BIOS program searches for and loads an OS.

QUESTION 146

The four system resources on a motherboard that the OS and processor use to interact with hardware are IRQ lines, I/O addresses, memory addresses, and the following:

A. DMA channels
B. Startup BIOS
C. CMOS RAM
D. PCI slots

EXPLANATION

The four system resources on a motherboard that the OS and processor use to interact with hardware are IRQ lines, I/O addresses, memory addresses, and DMA channels.

QUESTION 147

The following term defines a line of a motherboard bus that a hardware device or expansion slot can use to signal the CPU that the device needs attention:

A. I/O address
B. IRQ number
C. Memory address
D. DMA channels

EXPLANATION

The IRQ number is a line of a motherboard bus that a hardware device or expansion slot can use to signal the CPU that the device needs attention.

QUESTION 148

The following term defines numbers assigned to hardware devices that software uses to send a command to a device.

A. I/O addresses
B. Memory addresses
C. IRQ numbers
D. DMA channels

EXPLANATION

I/O addresses are numbers assigned to hardware devices that software uses to send a command to a device.

QUESTION 149

The following term refers to numbers assigned to physical memory located either in RAM or ROM chips:
   A. IRQ numbers
   B. DMA channels
   C. I/O addresses
   D. Memory addresses

EXPLANATION

Memory addresses are numbers assigned to physical memory located either in RAM or ROM chips.

QUESTION 150

The following term refers to a number designating a channel on which the device can pass data to memory without involving the CPU:
   A. I/O address
   B. IRQ number
   C. DMA channel
   D. Memory address

EXPLANATION

A DMA channel is a number designating a channel on which the device can pass data to memory without involving the CPU.

QUESTION 151

What is the memory address assigned to the first instruction in the ROM BIOS startup program?
   A. FFFF0h
   B. FFFF1h
   C. FFFF6h
   D. FFFFFh

EXPLANATION

FFFF0h is the memory address always assigned to the first instruction in the ROM BIOS startup program.

QUESTION 152

What is the name of the sector designated as the "beginning" of the hard drive?
A. Partition table
B. Boot record
C. Master Boot Record (MBR)
D. Program file

EXPLANATION

Even though a hard drive is a circular affair, it must begin somewhere. On the outermost track, one sector (512 bytes) is designated the "beginning" of the hard drive. This sector is called the Master Boot Record (MBR).

QUESTION 153

The following component has a map to the partitions on the hard drive:
A. Ntldr
B. Partition table
C. Program file
D. Io.sys

EXPLANATION

The second item in the MBR is a table, called the partition table, which contains a map to the partitions on the hard drive.

QUESTION 154

The following component loads the first program file of the OS:
A. MBR
B. Partition table
C. Active partition
D. OS boot record

EXPLANATION

At the beginning of the boot drive (usually drive C) is the OS boot record, which loads the first program file of the OS.

QUESTION 155

The following is a question you should ask when interviewing a user about a PC problem you are troubleshooting:

   A. What programs or software were you using?
   B. Why were you not using the company's antivirus software?
   C. Why were you not using a personal firewall program?
   D. Why did you move your computer across the room without authorization?

EXPLANATION

You can learn much about the problem by asking a question such as, What programs or software were you using? (Possible answer: I was using Internet Explorer.)

QUESTION 156

The following is a question you should ask when interviewing a user about a PC problem you are troubleshooting:

   A. Why did you move your computer across the room without authorization?
   B. Why did you install that hardware without authorization?
   C. Did you know that you cannot use that particular hardware?
   D. Did you move your computer recently?

EXPLANATION

You can learn much about the problem by asking a question such as, Did you move your computer system recently? (Possible answer: Well, yes. Yesterday I moved the computer case across the room.)

QUESTION 157

The following is a question you should ask when interviewing a user about a PC problem you are troubleshooting:

   A. Did you back up your data, because it is not my problem if you didn't?
   B. Can you show me how to reproduce the problem?
   C. Why did you install that hardware without authorization?
   D. Do you know what a Master Boot Record is?

EXPLANATION

You can learn much about the problem by asking a question such as, Can you show me how to reproduce the problem? (Possible answers: Yes, let me show you what to do.)

1

QUESTION 158

The following is true when troubleshooting a PC problem:
- A. Always blame the user
- B. Make the user feel belittled
- C. A good PC support technician knows how to interact with a user
- D. Make the user feel talked down to

EXPLANATION

A good PC support technician knows how to interact with a user so that the user gains confidence in your skills and does not feel talked down to or belittled.

QUESTION 159

The following is true when troubleshooting a PC problem:
- A. All PC problems are complex to solve
- B. Most PC problems are complex to solve
- C. All PC problems are simple and can be simply solved
- D. Most PC problems are simple and can be simply solved

EXPLANATION

Most PC problems are simple and can be simply solved, but you do need a game plan. After you've discovered the problem, many times the solution is obvious.

QUESTION 160

The following number of beeps during POST means motherboard problems, possibly with DMA, CMOS setup chip, or the system bus:
- A. Two beeps
- B. Continuous beeps
- C. One beep followed by three, four, or five beeps
- D. Four beeps followed by two, three, or four beeps

EXPLANATION

One beep followed by three, four, or five beeps means motherboard problems, possibly with DMA, CMOS setup chip, or the system bus. Most likely the motherboard will need to be replaced.

QUESTION 161

The following number of beeps means the first 64K of RAM has errors:
  A. Two beeps
  B. Two beeps followed by three, four, or five beeps
  C. One beep followed by three, four, or five beeps
  D. Four beeps followed by two, three, or four beeps

EXPLANATION

Two beeps followed by three, four, or five beeps means the first 64K of RAM has errors.

QUESTION 162

The following number of beeps means problems with the power supply:
  A. Continuous beeps
  B. One beep followed by three, four, or five beeps
  C. Two beeps followed by three, four, or five beeps
  D. Two beeps

EXPLANATION

Continuous beeps indicate a problem with the power supply. The power supply might need to be replaced.

QUESTION 163

The following type of systems satisfy certain energy-conserving standards of the U.S. Environmental Protection Agency (EPA):
  A. Green Leaf
  B. Energy Peace
  C. Green Peace
  D. Energy Star

EXPLANATION

Energy Star systems and peripherals have the U.S. Green Star, indicating that they satisfy certain energy-conserving standards of the U.S. Environmental Protection Agency (EPA).

1

QUESTION 164

The following standards generally mean that the computer or the device has a standby program that switches the device to sleep mode when it is not in use:
A. Green Standards
B. Star Standards
C. Sleep Standards
D. Power Standards

EXPLANATION

Energy Star standards, sometimes called the Green Standards, generally mean that the computer or the device has a standby program that switches the device to sleep mode when it is not in use.

QUESTION 165

How many watts of power should a device consume during sleep mode?
A. No more than 15 watts
B. No more than 30 watts
C. Exactly 45 watts
D. More than 60 watts

EXPLANATION

During sleep mode, the device must use no more than 30 watts of power.

QUESTION 166

The following is a set of standards that enables the BIOS to communicate with the OS about what hardware is present, what energy-saving features are present, and how they can be used:
A. Sleep Star
B. Display Power Management Signaling (DPMS)
C. Advanced Configuration and Power Interface (ACPI)
D. AT Attachment (ATA)

EXPLANATION

Advanced Configuration and Power Interface (ACPI), used with Windows 2000/XP and Windows 98/Me and supported by the system BIOS, is a set of standards that enable the BIOS to communicate with the OS about what hardware is present, what energy-saving features are present, and how they can be used.

QUESTION 167

The following energy-saving method allows hard drives and other type drives to stop spinning when they are not in use:
   A. AT Attachment (ATA)
   B. Advanced Power Management (APM)
   C. Display Power Management Signaling (DPMS)
   D. AT Star

EXPLANATION

AT Attachment (ATA) for hard drives and other type drives allows drives to stop spinning when they are not in use.

QUESTION 168

What is the current energy-saving standard used by most desktop and notebook computers?
   A. DPMS
   B. ACPI
   C. APM
   D. ATA

EXPLANATION

ACPI is the current standard used by most desktop and notebook computers.

QUESTION 169

In the following ACPI mode, the hard drive and monitor are turned off, and everything else runs normally:
   A. ATA-1
   B. D0
   C. S1
   D. S2

EXPLANATION

In S1 mode, the hard drive and monitor are turned off, and everything else runs normally.

QUESTION 170

What is the ACPI mode called hibernation?
   A. S1
   B. S2
   C. S3
   D. S4

1

EXPLANATION

S4 mode is called hibernation.

QUESTION 171

To manage power features in Windows, open the following applet from the Control Panel:

A. Network Connections
B. Power Options
C. Display Power Management Signaling (DPMS)
D. ACPI

EXPLANATION

To manage power features in Windows, go to the Control Panel and open the Power Options applet.

QUESTION 172

To control power using the BIOS, use the following menu from the CMOS setup:

A. DPMS
B. ACPI
C. APM
D. Power

EXPLANATION

To control power using the BIOS, go to CMOS setup and access the Power menu.

QUESTION 173

ACPI stores information that it needs to pass on to the OS in a series of tables. The master table is called:

A. Root System Description Table (RSDT)
B. ACPI MBR
C. ACPI FAT
D. ACPI OS Table

EXPLANATION

ACPI stores information that it needs to pass on to the OS in a series of tables. The master table is the Root System Description Table (RSDT).

QUESTION 174

The following controller can sometimes solve problems with devices not coming out of a sleep state correctly:

A. RSDT
B. ATA
C. APIC
D. APM

EXPLANATION

The APIC (Advanced Programmable Interrupt Controller) can sometimes solve problems with devices not coming out of a sleep state correctly.

QUESTION 175

What should the temperature be inside a computer case?

A. Less than 20 degrees F
B. Less than 50 degrees F
C. Less than 75 degrees F
D. Less than 100 degrees F

EXPLANATION

The temperature inside the case should never exceed 100 degrees F (38 degrees C).

QUESTION 176

The following is true:

A. Processors do not generate heat
B. All processors generate heat but do not need a cooler
C. Most processors require a cooler
D. Most processors do not generate heat but require a cooler

EXPLANATION

Most processors require a cooler with a fan installed on top of the processor.

QUESTION 177

The following is true about video cards:

A. AGP video cards do not generate heat
B. AGP video cards generate a lot of heat
C. Most AGP video cards generate heat
D. Some AGP video cards generate heat

1

EXPLANATION

An AGP video card generates a lot of heat. Make sure that you leave the PCI slot next to the AGP slot open to better ventilate the AGP card.

QUESTION 178

The following can damage the CPU and the motherboard:
A. Excessive heat
B. Low humidity
C. Cool temperature
D. Correct power supply

EXPLANATION

Excessive heat may damage the CPU and the motherboard.

QUESTION 179

What is the processor component that does all comparisons and calculations?
A. I/O unit
B. Control unit
C. ALU
D. Manager unit

EXPLANATION

The ALU does all comparisons and calculations.

QUESTION 180

What was the first processor used in an IBM PC?
A. 8080
B. 8088
C. 80286
D. 80386

EXPLANATION

The first processor used in an IBM PC was the 8088.

QUESTION 181

The following term refers to installing more than one processor on a motherboard:
A. Multiprocessor platform
B. Itanium
C. ALU
D. Dual-core

EXPLANATION

A method of improving performance is installing more than one processor on a motherboard, creating a multiprocessor platform.

QUESTION 182

The following term refers to the static RAM of a computer:

   A. DRAM

   B. Main memory

   C. Memory cache

   D. SROM

EXPLANATION

A memory cache is a small amount of RAM (referred to as static RAM [SRAM]) that is much faster than the rest of RAM, which is called dynamic RAM (DRAM).

QUESTION 183

The following term refers to a memory cache on the processor chip:

   A. DRAM

   B. Internal cache

   C. L5 cache

   D. SRAM

EXPLANATION

A memory cache on the processor chip is called an internal cache, a primary cache, or a Level 1 (L1) cache.

QUESTION 184

Some processors use the following type of cache containing a list of operations that have been decoded and are waiting to be executed:

   A. L2 cache

   B. Primary cache

   C. External cache

   D. Execution trace cache

EXPLANATION

The Pentium 4 has 8 K of Level 1 cache used for data and an additional 12 K of execution trace cache containing a list of operations that have been decoded and are waiting to be executed.

QUESTION 185

The following type of cache makes it possible for the Pentium to fit on a smaller and less expensive form factor:

A. Execution trace cache (ETC)

B. L1 cache

C. Advanced transfer cache (ATC)

D. L3 cache

EXPLANATION

ATC makes it possible for the Pentium to fit on a smaller and less expensive form factor.

QUESTION 186

What is the name of the new instruction set used by the Intel Itaniums processor?

A. Microcode

B. Explicitly parallel instruction computing (EPIC)

C. Reduced instruction set computing (RISC)

D. Complex instruction set computing (CISC)

EXPLANATION

The Intel Itaniums use a new instruction set called explicitly parallel instruction computing (EPIC).

QUESTION 187

The following term refers to a process that allows the CPU to receive a single instruction and then execute it on multiple pieces of data rather than receiving the same instruction each time each piece of data is received.

A. Multimedia Extensions (MMX)

B. Complex instruction set computing (CISC)

C. Single instruction, multiple data (SIMD)

D. Reduced instruction set computing (RISC)

EXPLANATION

SIMD, which stands for "single instruction, multiple data," is a process that allows the CPU to receive a single instruction and then execute it on multiple pieces of data rather than receiving the same instruction each time each piece of data is received.

QUESTION 188

How many ALUs does a Pentium processor have?

A. 2

B. 3

C. 4

D. 5

EXPLANATION

A Pentium has two ALUs, so it can perform two calculations at once; it is, therefore, a true multiprocessor.

QUESTION 189

The following processor is a low-end Pentium processor that targets the low-end PC multimedia and home market segments:

A. Pentium IV

B. Pentium M

C. Xeon

D. Celeron

EXPLANATION

The Celeron processor is a low-end Pentium processor that targets the low-end PC multimedia and home market segments.

QUESTION 190

What processor architecture was used by the first Pentium 4 processors to increase performance for multimedia applications?

A. Microcode

B. Explicitly parallel instruction computing (EPIC)

C. NetBurst

D. Multimedia Extensions (MMX)

EXPLANATION

The first Pentium 4 processors increased performance for multimedia applications such as digital video, as well as for new Web technologies, using a processor architecture that Intel calls NetBurst.

QUESTION 191

The following Intel processor is designed to be used on servers and high-end workstations in a corporate environment.
A. Pentium M
B. Xeon
C. Mobile Pentium 4
D. Pentium V

EXPLANATION

Xeons use Hyper-Threading Technology and dual-core processing and are designed to be used on servers and high-end workstations in a corporate environment.

QUESTION 192

What is another name for the current processor socket?
A. Pin grid array (PGA)
B. Staggered pin grid array (SPGA)
C. Land grid array (LGA)
D. Zero insertion force (ZIF)

EXPLANATION

Current processor sockets, called zero insertion force (ZIF) sockets, have a small lever on the side that lifts the processor up and out of the socket.

QUESTION 193

The fast end of the hub interface architecture, which contains the graphics and memory controller, connects to the system bus and is called:
A. South Bridge
B. Top Bridge
C. North Bridge
D. Bottom Bridge

EXPLANATION

The fast end of the hub, which contains the graphics and memory controller, connects to the system bus and is called the hub's North Bridge.

QUESTION 194

The following is true about chipsets and processors:
    A. Chipsets generate more heat than processors
    B. Chipsets generate less heat than processors
    C. Chipsets and processors generate the same heat
    D. Chipsets do not generate heat

EXPLANATION

Chipsets generate heat, but not as much heat as a processor generates.

QUESTION 195

Access to a computer can be secured using the following:
    A. Startup password
    B. SRAM
    C. Power-on RAM
    D. User RAM

EXPLANATION

Access to a computer can be controlled using a startup password, sometimes called a user password or power-on password.

QUESTION 196

The following CMOS setting sets the appropriate core voltage for the processor:
    A. Processor operating speed
    B. Core voltage
    C. External clock
    D. I/O voltage

EXPLANATION

The Core voltage option sets the appropriate core voltage for the processor.

QUESTION 197

What is the most reliable way to restore customized CMOS settings?
    A. Using CMOS RAM
    B. Using CMOS ROM
    C. Keeping a written record of all the changes
    D. Using an I/O voltage meter

EXPLANATION

The most reliable way to restore settings is to keep a written record of all the changes you make to CMOS.

QUESTION 198

The following is a third-party utility that allows you to save CMOS settings:

A. McAfee Internet Suite
B. ZoneAlarm Pro
C. Partition Magic
D. Norton Utilities

EXPLANATION

One third-party utility that allows you to save CMOS settings is Norton Utilities by Symantec (www.symantec.com).

QUESTION 199

The following term describes the process of upgrading or refreshing the ROM BIOS chip:

A. Startup BIOS
B. CMOSing BIOS
C. Flashing ROM
D. Flashing RAM

EXPLANATION

The process of upgrading or refreshing the ROM BIOS chip is called flashing ROM.

QUESTION 200

The following is a standard for communication between a subsystem of peripheral devices and the system bus:

A. SCSI
B. CMOS
C. BIOS
D. SPCI

EXPLANATION

SCSI (pronounced "scuzzy") stands for Small Computer System Interface and is a standard for communication between a subsystem of peripheral devices and the system bus.

QUESTION 201

What is the name of the adapter card responsible for managing all devices on the SCSI bus?

A. ATA SCSI
B. SCSI root
C. SCSI slot
D. Host adapter

EXPLANATION

The adapter card, called the host adapter, is responsible for managing all devices on the SCSI bus.

QUESTION 202

On a SCSI subsystem, each device is assigned a number from 0 to 15 called:
   A. Bus ID
   B. SCSI ID
   C. Logic Unit Number (LUN)
   D. Host ID

EXPLANATION

Each device on the bus is assigned a number from 0 to 15 called the SCSI ID, by means of DIP switches, dials on the device, or software settings.

QUESTION 203

The following component is used to reduce the amount of electrical "noise," or interference, on a SCSI cable:
   A. Terminating resistor
   B. Cable end
   C. Cable resistor
   D. Dual-voltage resistor

EXPLANATION

To reduce the amount of electrical "noise," or interference, on a SCSI cable, each end of the SCSI chain has a terminating resistor.

QUESTION 204

SCSI standards are developed by the following Technical Committee:
   A. ISO
   B. SCSI T10
   C. IETF 1
   D. IEEE 811

EXPLANATION

SCSI standards are developed by the SCSI T10 Technical Committee (www.t10.org) and sent to ANSI.

QUESTION 205

Which SCSI version is also known as Regular SCSI?
  A. ATA SCSI
  B. SCSI-0
  C. SCSI-1
  D. SAS

EXPLANATION

The three major versions of SCSI are SCSI-1, SCSI-2, and SCSI-3, commonly known as Regular SCSI, Fast SCSI, and Ultra SCSI.

QUESTION 206

Which SCSI version allows for more than 15 devices on a single SCSI chain?
  A. SCSI-0
  B. SCSI-1
  C. SCSI-3
  D. Serial SCSI

EXPLANATION

The latest SCSI standard, serial SCSI, also called serial attached SCSI (SAS), allows for more than 15 devices on a single SCSI chain.

QUESTION 207

The following software lets you manage partitions on a hard drive more quickly and easily than with Fdisk for Windows 9x/Me or Disk Management for Windows 2000/XP:
  A. UnErased Wizard
  B. PartitionMagic by Symantec
  C. Norton Internet Security
  D. GetDataBack by Runtime Software

EXPLANATION

PartitionMagic by Symantec (www.symantec.com) lets you manage partitions on a hard drive more quickly and easily than with Fdisk for Windows 9x/Me or Disk Management for Windows 2000/XP.

QUESTION 208

Seagate offers the following tools that can be used to create a bootable CD or floppy that can test and analyze most ATA and SCSI drives by Seagate and other manufacturers:

A. GetDataBack
B. PartitionMagic
C. SeaTools
D. Norton Utilities

EXPLANATION

Seagate offers SeaTools that can be downloaded and used to create a bootable CD or floppy to test and analyze most ATA and SCSI drives by Seagate and other manufacturers.

QUESTION 209

The following is true about hard drives:

A. A bad power supply has no relation to disk boot failures
B. A bad power supply does not affect SCSI hard drives
C. A bad motherboard does not affect SCSI hard drives
D. A bad power supply might cause a disk boot failure

EXPLANATION

A bad power supply or a bad motherboard might cause a disk boot failure.

QUESTION 210

The following message means the system BIOS cannot read the partition table information:

A. Invalid drive or drive specification
B. Drive cannot be recovered
C. Hard drive crash
D. Replace SCSI bus

EXPLANATION

If you get the error message "Invalid drive or drive specification," the system BIOS cannot read the partition table information.

1

QUESTION 211

The following type of I/O device includes expansion cards inserted in expansion slots on the motherboard:

A. Expansion device

B. External device

C. Internal device

D. Chipset device

EXPLANATION

Internal devices can also be expansion cards inserted in expansion slots on the motherboard.

QUESTION 212

The following is true about I/O devices:

A. Every I/O device is controlled by software

B. Only external I/O devices are controlled by software

C. Only internal I/O devices are controlled by software

D. All devices need application software to use the device

EXPLANATION

Every I/O device is controlled by software. When you install a new I/O device, such as a modem or printer, you must install both the device and the device drivers to control the device.

QUESTION 213

The following type of device allows you to move a pointer on the screen and perform tasks such as executing (clicking) a command button:

A. Keyboard

B. Pointing device

C. Internal device

D. Expansion device

EXPLANATION

A pointing device allows you to move a pointer on the screen and perform tasks such as executing (clicking) a command button.

QUESTION 214

The following type of mouse replaces the ball in a standard mouse with a microchip, miniature red light or laser light, and camera:

A. Track ball
B. Camera mouse
C. Ball mouse
D. Optical mouse

EXPLANATION

An optical mouse replaces the ball in a standard mouse with a microchip, miniature red light or laser light, and camera.

QUESTION 215

The following term describes a mouse that connects to the computer using a round PS/2 mouse port coming directly from the motherboard:

A. Motherboard mouse
B. Optical mouse
C. Bus mouse
D. Serial mouse

EXPLANATION

The mouse is called a motherboard mouse or PS/2-compatible mouse if it connects to the computer using a round PS/2 mouse port coming directly from the motherboard.

QUESTION 216

The following type of mouse requires a serial port and an IRQ for that port:

A. Optical mouse
B. Motherboard mouse
C. Bus mouse
D. Serial mouse

EXPLANATION

The serial mouse requires a serial port and an IRQ for that port.

QUESTION 217

The following type of input device uses a monitor or LCD panel as the backdrop for input options:

A. Keyboard
B. Touch screen
C. Tablet PC
D. Optical screen

1

EXPLANATION

A touch screen is an input device that uses a monitor or LCD panel as the backdrop for input options.

QUESTION 218

The following type of pointing device allows you to duplicate mouse function, moving the pointer by applying light pressure with one finger somewhere on a pad that senses the x, y movement:

A. Trackball
B. Touch screen
C. Touch pad
D. Optical mouse

EXPLANATION

A touch pad allows you to duplicate mouse function, moving the pointer by applying light pressure with one finger somewhere on a pad that senses the x, y movement.

QUESTION 219

The following is true about fingerprint readers:

A. They cannot use a wireless connection
B. They cannot use a USB connection
C. They cannot be embedded in other devices such as a keyboard
D. They can look like a mouse

EXPLANATION

Fingerprint readers can look like a mouse and use a wireless or USB connection.

QUESTION 220

A serial port conforms to the following interface standard:

A. IEEE 1394
B. SCSI
C. RS-232c
D. SATA

EXPLANATION

A serial port conforms to the interface standard called RS-232c (Reference Standard 232 revision c).

QUESTION 221

The following is an older type of cable that uses serial ports to connect two computers so they can communicate:

A. Null modem
B. IEEE 1394
C. STP
D. UTP

EXPLANATION

A null modem cable is an older type of cable that uses serial ports to connect two computers so they can communicate.

QUESTION 222

When a serial port is used by an external modem, the serial port is called:

A. Data Communication Equipment
B. Data Terminal Equipment
C. Data Server Equipment
D. Data Client Equipment

EXPLANATION

When a serial port is used by an external modem, in documentation, the serial port is called the DTE (Data Terminal Equipment).

QUESTION 223

The following component provides an infrared port for wireless communication:

A. USB antenna
B. FireWire transceiver
C. IR transceiver
D. Optical antenna

EXPLANATION

An infrared transceiver, also called an IrDA (Infrared Data Association) transceiver or an IR transceiver, provides an infrared port for wireless communication.

QUESTION 224

The following term refers to the logic on the motherboard that controls the serial ports on the board and is sometimes referred to as the UART 16550.

A. IEEE 1394
B. UART
C. IrDA
D. SATA

EXPLANATION

UART (universal asynchronous receiver-transmitter) refers to the logic on the motherboard that controls the serial ports on the board and is sometimes referred to as the UART 16550.

QUESTION 225

The following body defines infrared standards:

A. ANSI

B. IEEE

C. IETF

D. IrDA

EXPLANATION

Infrared standards are defined by the Infrared Data Association (IrDA).

QUESTION 226

The following radio technology is becoming the most popular way to connect a wireless I/O device to a nearby computer:

A. Bluetooth

B. FireWire

C. WiMAX

D. WiFi

EXPLANATION

Short-range radio technology such as Bluetooth is becoming the most popular way to connect a wireless I/O device to a nearby computer.

QUESTION 227

ECP was designed to increase speed over EPP by using the following:

A. FireWire bus

B. DMA channel

C. IR transceiver

D. Optical antenna

EXPLANATION

ECP was designed to increase speed over EPP by using a DMA channel.

QUESTION 228

If the parallel port is coming directly off the motherboard, use the following to configure the port:

A. CMOS setup

B. BIOS

C. SRAM

D. DDL configuration

EXPLANATION

If the parallel port is coming directly off the motherboard, use CMOS setup to configure the port.

QUESTION 229

FireWire and i.Link are common names for a peripheral bus officially named:

A. USB

B. Bluetooth

C. IEEE 1394

D. IrDA

EXPLANATION

FireWire and i.Link are common names for a peripheral bus officially named IEEE 1394.

QUESTION 230

What is the maximum speed supported by IEEE 1394b?

A. 600 Mbps

B. 1.2 Gbps

C. 2.3 Gbps

D. 3.2 Gbps

EXPLANATION

1394b supports speeds up to 3.2 Gbps, but current devices on the market are running at only 800 Mbps, which is why 1394b is also called FireWire 800.

QUESTION 231

The following term means that data is transferred continuously without breaks:

A. Isochronous data transfer

B. Peer-to-peer data transfer

C. Point-to-point data transfer

D. DMA data transfer

EXPLANATION

IEEE 1394 uses isochronous data transfer, meaning that data is transferred continuously without breaks.

QUESTION 232

The following term means you don't have to set jumpers or DIP switches on the card to use system resources:
A. PCI Express
B. ISA Express
C. AGP
D. PnP

EXPLANATION

Plug and Play (PnP) means you don't have to set jumpers or DIP switches on the card to use system resources, and installations should be easy to do using the Windows Found New Hardware Wizard.

QUESTION 233

The following is a device used by a PC to communicate over a phone line:
A. Mouse
B. Modem
C. Digital slot
D. Hub

EXPLANATION

A modem is a device used by a PC to communicate over a phone line.

QUESTION 234

What is the most common modem speed?
A. 12 Kbps
B. 36.4 Kbps
C. 56.6 Kbps
D. 61.3 Kbps

EXPLANATION

Modems are rated by speed; the most common modem speed is 56.6 Kbps.

QUESTION 235

The following is true when troubleshooting keyboards:
   A. Use rubbing alcohol to clean the keys well
   B. If the keyboard does not seem to work, just replace it
   C. Always use abundant water to clean a dirty keyboard
   D. Do not use rubbing alcohol to clean the keys

EXPLANATION

Don't use rubbing alcohol to clean the key well, because it can leave a residue on the contact.

QUESTION 236

The following is true when troubleshooting a keyboard:
   A. Always turn off the computer before plugging in the keyboard
   B. Do not turn off the PC before plugging in the keyboard
   C. Keyboards do not need to be detected during the boot
   D. Keyboards are not detected during the boot

EXPLANATION

Always power down a PC before plugging in a keyboard. The keyboard must be detected during the boot.

QUESTION 237

The following is true when troubleshooting a touch screen:
   A. Scratches do not affect the screen
   B. Crumbs and other particles at the edges of the screen do not affect it
   C. Examine the screen for excessive scratches
   D. Use abundant water to clean a dirty touch screen

EXPLANATION

Examine the screen for excessive scratches. Too many scratches might mean the screen needs to be replaced.

QUESTION 238

What is the first thing you see on a PC screen when you turn it on?
   A. Motherboard chipset identifying itself
   B. Firmware on the video card identifying itself
   C. PCI slot firmware identifying itself
   D. Hard drive BIOS identifying itself

EXPLANATION

When you turn on your PC, the first thing you see on the screen is the firmware on the video card identifying itself.

QUESTION 239

The following term describes a logical group of computers and users that share resources, where administration, resources, and security on a workstation are controlled by that workstation:

A. Domain
B. Client/server
C. Workgroup
D. Peer-to-peer

EXPLANATION

A workgroup is a logical group of computers and users that share resources, where administration, resources, and security on a workstation are controlled by that workstation.

QUESTION 240

A workgroup uses the following networking model:

A. Peer-to-peer
B. Client/Server
C. Multicast
D. NOS

EXPLANATION

A workgroup uses a peer-to-peer networking model.

QUESTION 241

A Windows domain database is called the directory database or:

A. NOS database
B. SAM database
C. Talk database
D. DC database

EXPLANATION

A Windows domain database is called the directory database or the security accounts manager (SAM) database.

QUESTION 242

The following component holds the original Windows domain directory database:
  A. Secondary domain controller
  B. Backup domain controller
  C. Child domain controller
  D. Primary domain controller

EXPLANATION

The primary domain controller (PDC) holds the original directory database, and read-only copies are stored on backup domain controllers (BDCs).

QUESTION 243

In Windows 2000/XP, you can use the following tool to search for useful information about problems with a device:
  A. Device Manager
  B. Disk Management
  C. Disk Manager
  D. Device Report

EXPLANATION

You can use Device Manager to search for useful information about problems with the device.

QUESTION 244

In Windows 2000/XP, the following command displays information about digitally signed files:
  A. Signature.exe
  B. Sigfiles.exe
  C. Sign.exe
  D. Sigverif.exe

EXPLANATION

Type the Sigverif.exe command in the Run dialog box. This command displays information about digitally signed files.

QUESTION 245

The following is a window that consolidates several Windows 2000/XP administrative tools that you can use to manage the local PC or other computers on the network:

A. NOS

B. Computer Management

C. Device Manager

D. Disk Management

EXPLANATION

Computer Management is a window that consolidates several Windows 2000/XP administrative tools that you can use to manage the local PC or other computers on the network.

QUESTION 246

The following term defines a single window that contains one or more administrative tools such as Device Manager or Disk Management:

A. Snap-in

B. Applet

C. Console

D. Script

EXPLANATION

A console is a single window that contains one or more administrative tools such as Device Manager or Disk Management.

QUESTION 247

The following Windows 2000/XP component is a hierarchical database containing information about all the hardware, software, device drivers, network protocols, and user configuration needed by the OS and applications:

A. Registry

B. Control Panel

C. LDAP

D. SAM

EXPLANATION

The Windows 2000/XP registry is a hierarchical database containing information about all the hardware, software, device drivers, network protocols, and user configuration needed by the OS and applications.

QUESTION 248

The following Windows 2000/XP registry subtree contains information about software and the way software is configured:

A. HKEY_CURRENT_USER

B. HKEY_LOCAL_MACHINE

C. HKEY_CLASS_ROOT

D. HKEY_USERS

EXPLANATION

The HKEY_CLASS_ROOT subtree contains information about software and the way software is configured.

QUESTION 249

Physically, the Windows registry is stored in five files called:

A. Caves

B. Hives

C. Packages

D. Clusters

EXPLANATION

Physically, the registry is stored in five files called hives.

QUESTION 250

The following tool is used to control the Windows and third-party services installed on a Windows 2000/XP system:

A. Task Manager

B. Device Manager

C. System Management

D. Services console

EXPLANATION

The Services console is used to control the Windows and third-party services installed on a Windows 2000/XP system.

QUESTION 251

The following defines a user to Windows and records information about the user:

A. Registry

B. User account

C. Digital signature

D. Digital certificate

EXPLANATION

A user account defines a user to Windows and records information about the user, including the user name, the password used to access the account, groups to which the account belongs, and the rights and permissions assigned to the account.

QUESTION 252

When Windows 2000/XP is first installed, it automatically creates two local accounts, called:

    A. Global user accounts

    B. Local user accounts

    C. Remote user accounts

    D. Built-in user accounts

EXPLANATION

Windows 2000/XP automatically creates built-in user accounts.

QUESTION 253

In Windows 2000/XP, an account that is a member of the following group can back up and restore any files on the system regardless of their access privileges to these files:

    A. Limited Users

    B. Power Users

    C. Backup Operators

    D. Guests

EXPLANATION

An account that is a member of the Backup Operators group can back up and restore any files on the system regardless of their access privileges to these files.

QUESTION 254

In Windows 2000/XP, an account that is a member of the following group has read-write access only on its own folders, read-only access to most system folders, and no access to other users' data:

    A. Limited Users

    B. Power Users

    C. Administrator

    D. Guests

EXPLANATION

An account that is a member of the Limited Users group has read-write access only on its own folders, read-only access to most system folders, and no access to other users' data.

QUESTION 255

In Windows 2000/XP, a profile that applies to a group of users is called:
A. User profile
B. Roaming user profile
C. Mandatory user profile
D. Group profile

EXPLANATION

A profile that applies to a group of users is called a group profile.

QUESTION 256

The following type of profile is a roaming user profile that applies to all users in a user group, and individual users cannot change that profile:
A. Mandatory user
B. Global user
C. Remote user
D. Group

EXPLANATION

Mandatory user profile is a roaming user profile that applies to all users in a user group, and individual users cannot change that profile.

QUESTION 257

What is the maximum length of characters of a user name for Windows 2000/XP?
A. 10
B. 12
C. 15
D. 20

EXPLANATION

User names for Windows 2000/XP logon can consist of up to 15 characters.

QUESTION 258

How can you log on to a Windows 2000 system?
A. Press the power button
B. Press the Ctrl+Alt+Del keys
C. Press the Tab key
D. Press the Esc key

EXPLANATION

With Windows 2000, there is only one way to log on to the system: pressing the Ctrl+Alt+Del keys to open the logon window.

QUESTION 259

The following can help with the problem of losing encrypted data and Internet passwords when a user password is reset:
A. Forgotten password floppy disk
B. Forgotten profile state
C. Mandatory user profile
D. Profile pen drive

EXPLANATION

Because of the problem of losing encrypted data and Internet passwords when a user password is reset, each new user should create a forgotten password floppy disk for use in the event he or she forgets the password.

QUESTION 260

The following tool can be used to move user files and preferences from another PC to a new PC:
A. Computer Management console
B. User State Migration Tool
C. Remote user tool
D. Alien User Migration Tool

EXPLANATION

There are two tools that move user files and preferences from another PC to a new PC: the Files and Settings Transfer Wizard and the User State Migration Tool (USMT).

QUESTION 261

With the following Windows 2000/XP utility, you can schedule a batch routine, script, or program to run daily, weekly, monthly, or at certain events such as startup:
A. Cron
B. Tasking
C. Calendar
D. Task Scheduler

EXPLANATION

With the Windows 2000/XP Task Scheduler utility, you can schedule a batch routine, script, or program to run daily, weekly, monthly, or at certain events such as startup.

QUESTION 262

One way to manage what users can do and how the system can be used is by applying settings from the following console under Windows 2000/XP Professional:
   A. Device Manager
   B. User Accounts
   C. Group Policy
   D. User Policy

EXPLANATION

One way to manage what users can do and how the system can be used is by applying settings from the Group Policy console (Gpedit.msc) under Windows XP Professional and Windows 2000 Professional.

QUESTION 263

The following is an extra copy of a data or software file that you can use if the original file becomes damaged or destroyed:
   A. Disk cluster
   B. External drive
   C. Removable device
   D. Backup

EXPLANATION

A backup is an extra copy of a data or software file that you can use if the original file becomes damaged or destroyed.

QUESTION 264

Windows 2000/XP offers the following program to back up files and folders:
   A. Ntbackup.exe
   B. Chkdsk.exe
   C. Fdisk.exe
   D. Dskbckp.exe

EXPLANATION

Windows 2000/XP offers the Ntbackup.exe program to back up files and folders.

QUESTION 265

The following is true about backing up data:
   A. Data should be backed up after about every 2 to 3 hours of data entry
   B. Data should be backed up after about every 3 to 6 hours of data entry
   C. Data should be backed up after about every 4 to 10 hours of data entry
   D. Data should be backed up after about every 10 to 16 hours of data entry

EXPLANATION

Data should be backed up after about every 4 to 10 hours of data entry.

QUESTION 266

With the following Windows 2000/XP backup option, all files that have been created or changed since the last backup are backed up, and all files are marked as backed up:

A. Full backup

B. Incremental backup

C. Differential backup

D. Daily backup

EXPLANATION

With incremental backup, all files that have been created or changed since the last backup are backed up, and all files are marked as backed up.

QUESTION 267

In analog systems, the following measure is the difference between the highest and lowest frequency that a device can transmit:

A. Bandwidth

B. Cable length

C. Network size

D. Segment speed

EXPLANATION

In analog systems, bandwidth is the difference between the highest and lowest frequency that a device can transmit.

QUESTION 268

What is the maximum throughput speed for GSM mobile telephone service?

A. 4.5 Kbps

B. 9.6 to 14.4 Kbps

C. 56 Kbps

D. 64 to 128 Kbps

EXPLANATION

GSM mobile telephone service has a maximum throughput of 9.6 to 14.4 Kbps.

QUESTION 269

What is the maximum throughput speed of an X.25 network?
A. 9.6 Kbps
B. 14.4 Kbps
C. 56 Kbps
D. 128 Kbps

EXPLANATION

X.25 has a maximum throughput of 56 Kbps.

QUESTION 270

What is the maximum throughput speed for an 802.11b network?
A. Up to 1 Mbps
B. Up to 5 Mbps
C. Up to 7 Mbps
D. Up to 11 Mbps

EXPLANATION

An 802.11b wireless network has a throughput of up to 11 Mbps.

QUESTION 271

A PC makes a direct connection to a network by way of the following:
A. Port
B. Network adapter
C. Service
D. Link

EXPLANATION

A PC makes a direct connection to a network by way of a network adapter.

QUESTION 272

Data is transmitted on a network in pieces called:
A. Links
B. Loads
C. Bags
D. Packets

EXPLANATION

Data is transmitted on a network in pieces called packets, datagrams, or frames.

QUESTION 273

What is the most common and least expensive variety of twisted-pair cable?

A. STP

B. T1

C. UTP

D. STP-100

EXPLANATION

It comes in two varieties: unshielded twisted pair (UTP) cable and shielded twisted pair (STP) cable. UTP cable is the most common and least expensive.

QUESTION 274

The following type of cable is used by ThickNet Ethernet:

A. RG8

B. RG58

C. Thin coaxial

D. STP

EXPLANATION

Thick cabling (called RG8 cabling) is used by ThickNet Ethernet.

QUESTION 275

What are the two types of fiber-optic cable?

A. Thin and Thick

B. STP and UDP

C. RG58 and RG59

D. Single-mode and multimode

EXPLANATION

Fiber-optic cable comes in two types: single-mode (thin, difficult to connect, expensive, and best performing) and multimode (most popular).

QUESTION 276

The following network topology uses a logical bus for data delivery but is wired as a physical star:

A. Star bus topology

B. Star topology

C. Ring topology

D. Bus topology

EXPLANATION

The network configuration that uses a logical bus for data delivery but is wired as a physical star is an example of a star bus topology.

QUESTION 277

The following type of cable is used to connect a computer to a hub or switch:
- A. Crossover cable
- B. Crosslink cable
- C. Patch cable
- D. Host cable

EXPLANATION

A patch cable (also called a straight-through cable) is used to connect a computer to a hub or switch.

QUESTION 278

The following type of cable is used to connect two PCs:
- A. Patch cable
- B. Crossover cable
- C. Crosslink cable
- D. Node cable

EXPLANATION

A crossover cable is used to connect two PCs (when a hub or switch is not used) to make the simplest network of all.

QUESTION 279

The following device amplifies signals on a network:
- A. Repeater
- B. Attenuator
- C. Bridge
- D. Router

EXPLANATION

A repeater is a device that amplifies signals on a network.

1

QUESTION 280

The following type of network covers a limited geographical area and is popular in places where networking cables are difficult to install:

A. LAN
B. MAN
C. WAN
D. WLAN

EXPLANATION

A Wireless LAN (WLAN) covers a limited geographical area and is popular in places where networking cables are difficult to install.

QUESTION 281

The following is true about wireless networks:

A. They are always faster than wired networks
B. They tend to be slower than wired networks
C. Security is not a problem with wireless networks
D. They cannot be used in hotel rooms

EXPLANATION

Wireless networks tend to be slower than wired networks, especially when they are busy.

QUESTION 282

What is the frequency range used by 802.11a?

A. 1.1 GHz
B. 2.0 GHz
C. 5.0 GHz
D. 7.0 GHz

EXPLANATION

Another IEEE standard is 802.11a, which works in the 5.0-GHz frequency range.

QUESTION 283

The following type of network is a wireless network that is designed to cover a wide area and is made up of numerous cells, which are sometimes called radio cells:

A. Bluetooth
B. Infrared
C. 802.11b
D. Cellular WAN

EXPLANATION

A cellular network or cellular WAN is a wireless network that is designed to cover a wide area and is made up of numerous cells, which are sometimes called radio cells.

QUESTION 284

The following term means both persons in a conversation can talk or transmit at the same time:
  A. Single
  B. Half-duplex
  C. Full-duplex
  D. One-way

EXPLANATION

Full-duplex transmission means both persons in a conversation can talk or transmit at the same time.

QUESTION 285

The following is a proprietary networking protocol suite for Macintosh computers:
  A. NetBIOS
  B. AppleTalk
  C. AppleBEUI
  D. NetTalk

EXPLANATION

AppleTalk is a proprietary networking protocol suite for Macintosh computers by Apple Corporation.

QUESTION 286

The following occurs when an operating system–level protocol such as TCP/IP associates itself with a lower-level hardware protocol such as Ethernet:
  A. Binding
  B. Latching
  C. Hooking
  D. Gluing

EXPLANATION

Binding occurs when an operating system–level protocol such as TCP/IP associates itself with a lower-level hardware protocol such as Ethernet.

1

QUESTION 287

The following term describes a 32-bit address consisting of a series of four 8-bit numbers separated by periods:

A. MAC address
B. Physical address
C. IP address
D. NIC address

EXPLANATION

An IP address is a 32-bit address consisting of a series of four 8-bit numbers separated by periods.

QUESTION 288

The following term describes a private or corporate network that uses TCP/IP:

A. Intranet
B. Extranet
C. Internet
D. Domain net

EXPLANATION

An intranet is a private or corporate network that uses TCP/IP.

QUESTION 289

A Class A IP address supports the following total number of possible networks:

A. 12
B. 127
C. 16,000
D. 2 million

EXPLANATION

A Class A IP address supports up to 127 networks.

QUESTION 290

A Class C IP address supports the following number of possible IP addresses:

A. 12
B. 64
C. 128
D. 254

EXPLANATION

A Class C IP address supports up to 254 IP addresses.

QUESTION 291

The following term describes a group of four dotted decimal numbers that tells TCP/IP if a computer's IP address is on the same or a different network as another computer:

A. NIC address
B. Logical address
C. Subnet mask
D. Socket address

EXPLANATION

A subnet mask is a group of four dotted decimal numbers that tells TCP/IP if a computer's IP address is on the same or a different network as another computer.

QUESTION 292

The following term describes subnet masks that use either all ones or all zeroes in an octet:

A. Classless subnet mask
B. CIDR mask
C. MAC mask
D. Classful subnet mask

EXPLANATION

Subnet masks that use either all ones or all zeroes in an octet are called classful subnet masks.

QUESTION 293

The following type of IP addresses are used on private intranets that are isolated from the Internet:

A. Public IP address
B. Private IP address
C. Classless IP address
D. Classful IP address

EXPLANATION

Private IP addresses are IP addresses used on private intranets that are isolated from the Internet.

1

QUESTION 294

The server that manages dynamically assigned IP addresses is called:
  A. DHCP server
  B. CDIR server
  C. HTTP server
  D. SMTP server

EXPLANATION

The server that manages dynamically assigned IP addresses is called a DHCP (Dynamic Host Configuration Protocol) server

QUESTION 295

When a network card is installed in Windows 2000/XP, the following protocol suite is installed by default:
  A. AppleTalk
  B. NetBEUI
  C. IPX/SPX
  D. TCP/IP

EXPLANATION

When a network card is installed in Windows 2000/XP, TCP/IP is installed by default.

QUESTION 296

Windows 2000/XP makes shared resources available by way of:
  A. My Network Places
  B. Network Neighborhood
  C. My Shared Places
  D. My Documents

EXPLANATION

Windows 2000/XP makes shared resources available by way of My Network Places.

QUESTION 297

The following two Windows components must be installed before you can share resources:
  A. IPX/SPX and NetBIOS
  B. DNS and DHCP
  C. Client for Microsoft Networks and File and Printer Sharing
  D. DNS and Client for Microsoft Networks

EXPLANATION

Two Windows components must be installed before you can share resources: Client for Microsoft Networks and File and Printer Sharing.

QUESTION 298

The following Windows component allows you to use resources on the network made available by other computers:
   A. File and Printer Sharing
   B. Client for Microsoft Networks
   C. NetBIOS
   D. NetBEUI

EXPLANATION

Client for Microsoft Networks is the Windows component that allows you to use resources on the network made available by other computers.

QUESTION 299

The following Windows component allows you to share resources on your computer with others:
   A. File and Printer Sharing
   B. NetBEUI
   C. Client for Microsoft Networks
   D. TCP/IP

EXPLANATION

File and Printer Sharing allows you to share resources on your computer with others.

QUESTION 300

What is the key to successful wireless networking?
   A. Use of WiMAX
   B. Good cabling
   C. Use of Gigabit Ethernet
   D. Good security

EXPLANATION

The key to successful wireless networking is good security.

QUESTION 301

WPA encryption is also called:
- A. WEP encryption
- B. TKIP encryption
- C. 3DES encryption
- D. SHA encryption

EXPLANATION

WPA encryption is also called TKIP (Temporal Key Integrity Protocol) encryption.

QUESTION 302

A VPN uses the following technique in which a packet of data is encrypted:
- A. Socket
- B. Binding
- C. Tunneling
- D. Filtering

EXPLANATION

A VPN uses a technique called tunneling, in which a packet of data is encrypted.

QUESTION 303

The following technology uses an authentication server to control access to a network:
- A. DHCP
- B. RADIUS
- C. Client for Microsoft Networks
- D. Tunneling

EXPLANATION

RADIUS stands for Remote Authentication Dial-In User Service and uses an authentication server to control access.

QUESTION 304

The following tool helps to eliminate electromagnetic interference on a network cable:
- A. Ferrite clamp
- B. Grounded bracelet
- C. Grounded mat
- D. Grounded clamp

EXPLANATION

A ferrite clamp helps to eliminate electromagnetic interference.

QUESTION 305

What is the most useful Windows TCP/IP diagnostic tool?
  A. DHCP
  B. WPA
  C. Ping
  D. Getmac

EXPLANATION

Windows TCP/IP includes several diagnostic tools that are useful in troubleshooting problems with TCP/IP. The most useful is Ping (Packet Internet Groper).

QUESTION 306

The following Windows 2000/XP tool tests the TCP/IP configuration:
  A. Getmac
  B. Bindip
  C. Winipcfg
  D. Ipconfig

EXPLANATION

Ipconfig under Windows 2000/XP and Winipcfg under Windows 9x/Me test the TCP/IP configuration.

QUESTION 307

Most applications that use the Internet are the following type of application:
  A. Client/server
  B. Local
  C. PC
  D. Peer-to-peer

EXPLANATION

Most applications that use the Internet are client/server applications.

QUESTION 308

Commonly, the SSH protocol works on the following TCP/IP port:
  A. 15
  B. 22
  C. 80
  D. 110

EXPLANATION

SSH listens on the TCP/IP port 22.

QUESTION 309

The following protocol is responsible for locating a host on a local network:
  A. DHCP
  B. ICMP
  C. SMTP
  D. ARP

EXPLANATION

ARP (Address Resolution Protocol) is responsible for locating a host on a local network.

QUESTION 310

The following term refers to any type of networking medium that carries more than one type of transmission:
  A. Cable modem
  B. Broadband
  C. DSL
  D. Wi-Fi

EXPLANATION

Broadband refers to any type of networking medium that carries more than one type of transmission.

QUESTION 311

The following network equipment can filter data packets, examining the destination IP address or source IP address or the type of protocol used:
  A. Firewall
  B. Hub
  C. Repeater
  D. Access Point

EXPLANATION

A firewall can filter data packets, examining the destination IP address or source IP address or the type of protocol used.

QUESTION 312

Before Service Pack 2 for Windows XP was released, the firewall software for Windows XP was called:
  A. ZoneAlarm
  B. Internet Security
  C. Windows XP Internet Connection Firewall (ICF)
  D. Personal Firewall

EXPLANATION

Before Service Pack 2 for Windows XP was released, the firewall software for Windows XP was called Windows XP Internet Connection Firewall (ICF).

QUESTION 313

The following is the preferred Windows Firewall setting when you're traveling or using public networks or Internet connections:

A. Off
B. Don't allow exceptions
C. Allow exceptions
D. Disabled

EXPLANATION

"Don't allow exceptions" is the preferred setting when you're traveling or using public networks or Internet connections.

QUESTION 314

Which of the following is one of the encryption protocols supported by Windows XP for the VPN user account and password data?

A. L2TP
B. DES
C. SPAP
D. SSL

EXPLANATION

SPAP (Shiva Password Authentication Protocol) is one of the encryption protocols supported by Windows XP for the user account and password data.

QUESTION 315

To configure a VPN using Windows XP, a VPN network connection is created using the following window:

A. Personal Firewall
B. Windows Security Center
C. Personal Firewall Exceptions
D. Windows XP Network Connections

EXPLANATION

To configure a VPN using Windows XP, a VPN network connection is created using the Windows XP Network Connections window.

QUESTION 316

What type of encryption is used by default by Windows XP when creating a VPN client?
A. PPTP
B. L2TP
C. SSL
D. IPSec

EXPLANATION

Windows XP automatically uses PPTP encryption.

QUESTION 317

The following is a method to keep your computer secure:
A. When traveling, turn your personal firewall off
B. Don't use AV software
C. Keep Windows updates current
D. Set Microsoft Internet Explorer for minimal security

EXPLANATION

One way to secure your computer is to keep Windows updates current.

QUESTION 318

The following term refers to methods for determining what an individual can do in the system after he or she is authenticated:
A. Authority
B. Availability
C. Integrity
D. Authorization

EXPLANATION

Authorization determines what an individual can do in the system after he or she is authenticated.

QUESTION 319

AV software detects a known virus by looking for distinguishing characteristics called:
A. Virus signatures
B. Attack list
C. Attack patterns
D. Skeletons

EXPLANATION

AV software detects a known virus by looking for distinguishing characteristics called virus signatures.

QUESTION 320

The following is true about antivirus software:
   A. AV software can detect a virus it does not know
   B. AV software cannot always detect spyware and adware
   C. AV software can always stop spyware and adware
   D. If you have an antivirus software, you don't need an anti-adware software

EXPLANATION

Because AV software does not always stop adware or spyware, it's also a good idea to run anti-adware software in the background.

QUESTION 321

You can launch the Windows Update utility by entering the following command in the Run dialog box:
   A. wseccent.exe
   B. wsecpc.exe
   C. update.exe
   D. wupdmgr.exe

EXPLANATION

You can launch the Windows Update utility by entering wupdmgr.exe in the Run dialog box.

QUESTION 322

The following controls allow Web pages to execute program code on your machine:
   A. Script
   B. ActiveX
   C. MMX
   D. MMS

EXPLANATION

ActiveX controls allow Web pages to execute program code on your machine.

1

QUESTION 323

The following statement is true:
  A. Notebooks are more expensive than desktop PCs with similar features
  B. Desktop PCs are always more expensive than notebooks
  C. Desktop PCs and notebooks cannot be compared
  D. Notebooks are cheaper than desktop PCs with similar features

EXPLANATION

Notebooks and their replacement parts cost more than desktop PCs with similar features because their components are designed to be more compact and stand up to travel.

QUESTION 324

The following is true about notebooks and desktop PCs:
  A. Desktop computers tend to have a unique case
  B. Notebook computer cases tend to be similar to one another
  C. Every notebook has a unique case
  D. Notebooks do not have cases

EXPLANATION

Every notebook model has a unique case.

QUESTION 325

The following is a useful and interesting Web site that contains service manuals for several different brands of notebooks:
  A. www.notebooks.org
  B. www.eserviceinfo.com
  C. www.rarlab.com
  D. www.openingcases.com

EXPLANATION

One useful and interesting Web site that contains service manuals for several different brands of notebooks as well as service manuals for lots of other electronic devices is www.eserviceinfo.com.

QUESTION 326

The following is diagnostic software used by several Lenovo and IBM ThinkPad models:
  A. Panda
  B. PartitionMagic
  C. PC-Doctor
  D. Dr. Watson

EXPLANATION

One example of diagnostic software is PC-Doctor, which is used by several Lenovo and IBM ThinkPad models.

QUESTION 327

The following Windows 2000/XP feature allows you to use two modem connections at the same time to speed up data throughput when connected over phone lines:
   A. Channel aggregation
   B. Power management
   C. Support for PC cards
   D. Folder redirection

EXPLANATION

Channel aggregation allows you to use two modem connections at the same time to speed up data throughput when connected over phone lines.

QUESTION 328

The following Windows 2000/XP tool stores shared network files and folders in a cache on the notebook hard drive so that you can use them offline:
   A. Briefcase
   B. Folder redirection
   C. Hardware profiles
   D. Offline Files and Folders

EXPLANATION

Offline Files and Folders replaces Windows 9x/Me Briefcase and stores shared network files and folders in a cache on the notebook hard drive so that you can use them offline.

QUESTION 329

The following is a good notebook care guideline:
   A. Don't use antivirus software
   B. Connect to public networks without using a personal firewall
   C. Don't connect the notebook to a phone line during an electrical storm
   D. Tightly pack the notebook in a suitcase

EXPLANATION

Don't connect the notebook to a phone line during an electrical storm.

QUESTION 330

The following is true about cleaning a notebook:
- A. Clean the LCD panel with a soft wet cloth
- B. Don't clean the LCD panel
- C. Never remove the keyboard to clean under it
- D. It is not necessary to disassemble a notebook for routine cleaning

EXPLANATION

It is not necessary to disassemble a notebook for routine cleaning. In fact, you can clean the LCD panel, battery connections, keyboard, touch pad, or even memory contacts as needed without opening the notebook case.

QUESTION 331

The following is true about cleaning a notebook:
- A. Use compressed air to blow out all air vents
- B. Never clean air vents on a notebook
- C. Use a soft wet cloth to clean air vents on a notebook
- D. Never clean the LCD panel

EXPLANATION

Use compressed air to blow out all air vents on the notebook to make sure they are clean and unobstructed.

QUESTION 332

In Windows 2000/XP, you can change wireless settings using the following window:
- A. IExplorer
- B. Network Connections
- C. System Tray Properties
- D. Infrared Connections

EXPLANATION

To change wireless settings, use the Network Connections window.

QUESTION 333

By default, a wired or wireless network connection is set for the following type of addressing:
- A. Static IP
- B. Alternate IP
- C. Bluetooth IP
- D. Dynamic IP

EXPLANATION

By default, a wired or wireless network connection is set for dynamic IP addressing, which is the right choice for most public and corporate networks.

QUESTION 334

The following is true about Bluetooth:
  A. Windows XP Service Pack 1 is required for Bluetooth
  B. Windows XP Service Pack 2 is required for Bluetooth
  C. Windows XP Service Pack 2 does not support Bluetooth
  D. Windows XP Home Edition does not support Bluetooth

EXPLANATION

Windows XP Service Pack 2 is required for Bluetooth.

QUESTION 335

When working inside a notebook case, use the following tool to protect the system against ESD:
  A. Ground strap
  B. Alligator clamp
  C. Ferrita clamp
  D. Alligator strap

EXPLANATION

Before opening the case of a notebook or touching sensitive components, you should always use a ground strap to protect the system against ESD.

QUESTION 336

You will need the following tool to disassemble a notebook:
  A. Rubber hammer
  B. Magnetic screwdriver
  C. Torx screwdriver set
  D. Paper strap

EXPLANATION

You will need a Torx screwdriver set, particularly size T5, to disassemble a notebook.

QUESTION 337

Where should you dispose of a notebook backup battery?

A. Burn it

B. Take it to a recycle center

C. Bury it

D. Smash it before burning it

EXPLANATION

Dispose of a used backup battery by taking it to a recycle center.

QUESTION 338

Local printers and scanners connect directly to a computer using one of the following interfaces:

A. SATA port

B. ISA slot

C. USB port

D. PCI port

EXPLANATION

Local printers and scanners connect directly to a computer by way of a USB port.

QUESTION 339

The following type of printer creates a printed page by using some mechanism that touches or hits the paper:

A. Impact printer

B. Nonimpact printer

C. Soft printer

D. Hard printer

EXPLANATION

An impact printer creates a printed page by using some mechanism that touches or hits the paper.

QUESTION 340

What is the first step in the printing process for a laser printer?

A. Fusing

B. Conditioning

C. Writing

D. Cleaning

EXPLANATION

The first step in the printing process for a laser printer is cleaning.

QUESTION 341

What does Hewlett-Packard (HP) call the technology of varying the size of dots in a laser printer?
  A. REt
  B. DPI
  C. PLC
  D. PPM

EXPLANATION

Hewlett-Packard (HP) calls this technology of varying the size of dots REt (Resolution Enhancement technology).

QUESTION 342

In what step of the printing process for a laser printer does a strong electrical charge draw the toner off the drum onto the paper?
  A. Writing
  B. Transferring
  C. Developing
  D. Fusing

EXPLANATION

In the transferring step, a strong electrical charge draws the toner off the drum onto the paper.

QUESTION 343

What is the most common technology used by ink-jet printers?
  A. Ret jet
  B. Photo jet
  C. InkJet
  D. Bubble-jet

EXPLANATION

Ink-jet printer manufacturers use several technologies, but the most popular is the bubble-jet.

1

QUESTION 344

The following type of printer uses ink stored in solid blocks, which Xerox calls color sticks:

A. Laser printer
B. Thermal printer
C. Solid ink printer
D. Dye-sublimation printer

EXPLANATION

Solid ink printers use ink stored in solid blocks, which Xerox calls color sticks.

QUESTION 345

The following type of scanner works by using a motor that moves the scanning head across the paper placed on the glass bed of the scanner:

A. Portable scanner
B. Flat-bed scanner
C. Sheet-fed scanner
D. Laser scanner

EXPLANATION

A flat-bed scanner works by using a motor that moves the scanning head across the paper laid on the glass bed of the scanner.

QUESTION 346

The following is true when installing a local printer on a Windows 2000/XP system:

A. You must always use a wireless printer as a local printer
B. You cannot use a wireless printer as your local printer
C. You are asked if you want this printer to be the default printer
D. A local printer cannot be the default printer

EXPLANATION

The setup program asks if you want this printer to be the default printer. Click Yes or No to make your selection.

QUESTION 347

To use a shared printer on a remote PC, the following component must be installed:

A. Client for Microsoft Networks
B. File and Printer Sharing
C. Printing Client
D. Printing for Microsoft Sharing

EXPLANATION

To use a shared printer on a remote PC, Client for Microsoft Networks must be installed.

QUESTION 348

One way to install a network printer is to first use the following tool to locate the printer on the network:

A. Briefcase
B. Offline Files and Folders
C. Resource relocation
D. My Network Places

EXPLANATION

One way to install a shared printer is to first use My Network Places or Network Neighborhood to locate the printer on the network.

QUESTION 349

The following language, developed by Adobe Systems, is used to communicate the way a page is to print:

A. PostScript
B. PCL
C. GDI
D. DPI

EXPLANATION

PostScript, developed by Adobe Systems, is a language used to communicate the way a page is to print.

QUESTION 350

In Windows 2000/XP, the following permission level can be assigned to a user so that he or she can manage the print queue while not being allowed to change printer settings:

A. Print
B. Manage Printers
C. Manage Documents
D. Manage Spool

EXPLANATION

The Manage Documents permission level can be assigned to a user so that he or she can manage the print queue while not being allowed to change printer settings.

1

QUESTION 351

What is the most common type of connector for a scanner intended to be used with a desktop system?

A. SCSI

B. FireWire

C. Parallel

D. USB

EXPLANATION

The most common type of connector for a scanner intended to be used with a desktop system is a USB port.

QUESTION 352

The following is true when installing older scanners that use a serial or parallel port:

A. You can connect the scanner without powering your PC down

B. You must power your PC down before connecting the scanner

C. Parallel port scanners are not supported by Windows XP

D. Serial port scanners are not supported by Windows 2000

EXPLANATION

For older scanners that use a serial or parallel port, first power down your PC and connect the scanner.

QUESTION 353

What is probably the most significant indication that a PC technician is doing a good job?

A. The technician took too much time to solve the problem

B. The problem did not show up again

C. Customers are consistently satisfied

D. The technician took little time to solve the problem

EXPLANATION

Probably the most significant indication that a PC technician is doing a good job is that customers are consistently satisfied.

QUESTION 354

The following trait distinguishes one competent technician from another in the eyes of the customer:

A. Appears to be preoccupied
B. Has a positive and helpful attitude
C. Tries not to look overly professional
D. Is not customer-focused

EXPLANATION

One trait that distinguishes competent technicians in the eyes of the customer is a positive and helpful attitude. This helps establish good customer relationships.

QUESTION 355

The following trait distinguishes one competent technician from another in the eyes of the customer:

A. Never asks for help
B. Does not look like you need help
C. Constantly asks for help
D. If needed, asks for help

EXPLANATION

Credible technicians know when the job is beyond their expertise and when to ask for help.

QUESTION 356

The following characteristic constitutes good service in the eyes of most customers:

A. The technician responds and completes the work within a reasonable time
B. The work is done after several tries
C. The technician always recommends on-site visits
D. The problem is always solved after several on-site visits

EXPLANATION

The technician responds and completes the work within a reasonable time.

QUESTION 357

The following characteristic constitutes good service in the eyes of most customers:

A. The technician does not bother to inform the customer about the progress of the work
B. The technician exhibits good interpersonal skills
C. The technician seems extremely eager to finish the job
D. The technician uses the phone only to get the customer's information and immediately recommends an on-site visit

1

EXPLANATION

The technician exhibits good interpersonal skills.

QUESTION 358

The following is true when planning for good customer service:
  A. Be familiar with your company's customer service policies
  B. Be problem-focused
  C. Put your company's interests first
  D. Do not be too customer-focused

EXPLANATION

Be familiar with your company's customer service policies.

QUESTION 359

The following is true when planning for good customer service:
  A. Always recommend on-site visits
  B. Think of the big picture; try not to isolate the problem
  C. Never ask for help
  D. Check for user errors

EXPLANATION

Use your troubleshooting skills. Isolate the problem. Check for user errors.

QUESTION 360

The following is true when making an on-site service call:
  A. Ignore the urgency of the situation
  B. Be problem-focused
  C. Know the problem you are going to address
  D. Arrive without tools; your goal is to obtain information first

EXPLANATION

Know the problem you are going to address, the urgency of the situation, and what computer, software, and hardware need servicing.

QUESTION 361

The following is true when making an on-site service call:

A. Generally, use Mr. or Ms. and last names when addressing the customer
B. Ask the user to help you fill out the paperwork before you start working on the problem
C. Always use first names when addressing your customers
D. Do not start working until you have the formal description of the problem filled out on paper by the user

EXPLANATION

Use Mr. or Ms. and last names rather than first names when addressing the customer, unless you are certain the customer expects you to use first names.

QUESTION 362

The following is true when making an on-site service call:

A. You can use any customer's resources without asking permission
B. You only need to ask permission once to use the customer's resources
C. Don't use the phone without permission
D. You can use the customer's printer without asking permission

EXPLANATION

Don't use the phone or sit in the customer's desk chair without permission.

QUESTION 363

The following is true when interacting with the customer:

A. The less you ask the customer about the problem, the better
B. Ignore the customer's comments about the problem
C. Be problem-focused
D. Re-create the problem in as much detail as possible

EXPLANATION

Re-create the circumstances that existed when the computer stopped in as much detail as you can.

QUESTION 364

You suspect the customer dropped her PC. Which question would be appropriate to ask?

A. Are you responsible for dropping the PC?
B. Could the PC have been dropped?
C. Do you know who dropped the PC?
D. Do you know why the PC was dropped?

EXPLANATION

If you suspect that the user dropped the PC, don't ask, "Did you drop the PC?" Put the question in a less accusatory manner: "Could the PC have been dropped?"

QUESTION 365

The following is true when working at the user's desk:
   A. Explain to the customer that you need your space to work
   B. Ask the user to realize that solving the problem is the first priority
   C. Don't pile your belongings and tools on top of the user's papers
   D. It is acceptable to put your belongings and tools on top of the user's papers

EXPLANATION

Don't pile your belongings and tools on top of the user's papers, books, and so on.

QUESTION 366

The following is a good communication skill:
   A. Do not use direct statements
   B. Use clear, concise, and direct statements
   C. Customers like to be treated like peers, use techie language with them
   D. Ask the user for permission to take drastic actions before you start solving the problem; this way you won't need to consult the user every time

EXPLANATION

When talking, use clear, concise, and direct statements.

QUESTION 367

The following is true when selecting PC support tools:
   A. Tools should not include a ground bracelet
   B. A multimeter is an essential tool
   C. A flat-head screwdriver is not an essential tool
   D. Tools depend on the level of PC support you expect to provide

EXPLANATION

The tools you choose depend on the amount of money you can spend and the level of PC support you expect to provide.

QUESTION 368

The following tool might not be essential but is a convenient PC support tool:
A. Pen and paper
B. Ground bracelet
C. Tweezers
D. Recovery CD

EXPLANATION

Pen and paper for taking notes are convenient PC support tools.

QUESTION 369

You can find information about MSDSs at the following Web site:
A. www.microsoft.com/msds
B. www.ilpi.com/msds
C. www.safety.com/msds
D. www.safetyfirst.com/msds

EXPLANATION

You can find one on the Internet (see www.ilpi.com/msds).

QUESTION 370

The following is true about PC support tools:
A. A POST diagnostic card is not an essential tool
B. A multimeter is an essential tool
C. A magnetic screwdriver is an essential tool
D. A Torx screwdriver helps you discover errors and conflicts at POST

EXPLANATION

Although not an essential tool, a POST diagnostic card can be of great help to discover and report computer errors and conflicts at POST.

QUESTION 371

The following is true when physically protecting your computer:
A. It is okay to move your computer when it is powered on
B. Always leave your computer turned on
C. High humidity cannot damage your computer
D. Don't smoke around your computer

EXPLANATION

Don't smoke around your computer. For older hard drives that are not adequately sealed, smoke particles can get inside and crash a drive.

1

QUESTION 372

The following is true to obtain optimum airflow on your computer:
- A. Cover the entire case when the computer is powered on
- B. Leave empty expansion slots and bays uncovered
- C. Do not leave empty expansion slots and bays uncovered
- D. Block air vents on the front and rear of the computer case

EXPLANATION

For optimum airflow, don't leave empty expansion slots and bays uncovered.

QUESTION 373

The following is true when protecting private data:
- A. Store the data on a flash drive, and put the drive in a fire-proof safe
- B. Cryptography is enough to protect private data
- C. Encryption will protect your data from all threats
- D. If you encrypt your data, there is no need to put it under lock and key

EXPLANATION

Store the data on a removable storage device such as a flash drive and, when you're not using the data, put the flash drive in a fire-proof safe.

QUESTION 374

The following is true when unpacking hardware or software:
- A. Leave the cellophane on the working area
- B. Use the packing tape to protect it against static electricity
- C. Remove the packing tape and cellophane from the work area
- D. Use the cellophane to protect it against static electricity

EXPLANATION

When unpacking hardware or software, to help protect against static electricity, remove the packing tape and cellophane from the work area as soon as possible.

QUESTION 375

You should dispose of 9-volt batteries in the following way:
- A. Burn them
- B. Smash them
- C. Bury them
- D. Throw them in the trash

EXPLANATION

Dispose of these batteries in the regular trash. First check to see if there are recycling facilities in your area.

QUESTION 376

How should you dispose of ink-jet printer cartridges?
  A. Throw them in the trash
  B. Check local laws and regulations
  C. Burn them
  D. Bury them

EXPLANATION

Check with local county or environmental officials for laws and regulations in your area for proper disposal of these items.

QUESTION 377

The following is true when working inside a computer case:
  A. Use a graphite pencil to change DIP switch settings
  B. It is safe to work inside a modern computer case
  C. Never touch the inside of a computer that is turned on
  D. It is safe to stack boards on top of each other

EXPLANATION

Never touch the inside of a computer that is turned on.

QUESTION 378

The following is true when working inside a computer case:
  A. It is safe to place expansion cards next to a monitor
  B. Do not place or store expansion cards on top of or next to a monitor
  C. It is safe to place expansion cards on top of a monitor
  D. A monitor cannot damage components with ESD

EXPLANATION

Do not place or store expansion cards on top of or next to a monitor, which can discharge as much as 29,000 volts onto the screen.

QUESTION 379

If you can see the static charge, you discharged at least the following amount of volts of static electricity:

A. 10
B. 3,000
C. 6,000
D. 8,000

EXPLANATION

If you can see the discharge, you released at least 8,000 volts of ESD.

ANSWER GRID FOR COMPTIA A+ ESSENTIALS

Question	Answer	Objective	Question	Answer	Objective
1	C	1.1	35	A	3.1
2	D	1.1	36	D	3.1
3	A	1.1	37	B	3.1
4	D	1.1	38	C	3.1
5	C	4.1	39	B	3.1
6	C	1.1	40	A	3.1
7	D	1.1	41	C	3.3
8	C	1.1	42	D	3.1
9	B	1.1	43	A	3.1
10	B	1.1	44	D	3.1
11	A	1.1	45	B	3.1
12	A	1.1	46	C	3.1
13	D	1.2	47	D	3.1
14	B	1.1	48	B	3.1
15	C	1.2	49	B	3.1
16	B	1.1	50	A	3.1
17	C	1.1	51	C	3.1
18	D	1.1	52	A	3.1
19	C	1.1	53	B	3.1
20	D	1.1	54	D	3.1
21	B	1.1	55	A	3.3
22	A	1.1	56	C	3.1
23	C	1.1	57	D	3.1
24	B	1.1	58	B	3.1
25	A	1.1	59	B	3.1
26	D	1.4	60	C	3.1
27	D	3.1	61	D	3.1
28	A	3.2	62	A	3.1
29	D	3.1	63	D	3.1
30	B	3.1	64	B	3.1
31	C	3.1	65	A	3.1
32	D	3.1	66	C	3.1
33	A	3.1	67	C	3.1
34	B	3.1	68	B	3.1

Question	Answer	Objective	Question	Answer	Objective
69	D	3.1	105	A	2.4
70	A	3.1	106	A	2.4
71	C	3.1	107	C	2.4
72	A	3.1	108	B	2.4
73	D	3.1	109	A	2.4
74	B	3.1	110	D	2.4
75	A	1.1	111	A	6.1
76	B	1.1	112	B	6.1
77	D	1.1	113	D	7.2
78	C	1.1	114	C	7.2
79	D	3.1	115	D	7.2
80	B	3.1	116	A	7.2
81	C	1.2–1.3	117	C	7.2
82	A	3.1	118	B	7.2
83	B	3.1	119	D	7.2
84	A	3.1	120	B	7.2
85	C	3.1	121	C	7.2
86	D	3.1	122	A	7.2
87	C	3.1	123	C	1.2
88	B	3.1	124	A	1.2
89	D	3.1	125	B	1.2
90	A	7.1	126	D	1.2
91	D	7.1	127	A	1.2
92	B	7.1	128	D	1.2
93	A	7.1	129	C	1.2
94	C	7.1	130	B	1.2
95	B	6.1	131	D	1.2
96	C	6.1	132	B	1.2
97	A	7.1	133	A	1.2
98	D	2.4	134	C	1.2
99	C	2.4	135	B	1.2
100	D	2.4	136	D	1.3
101	B	6.1–6.3	137	C	1.3
102	A	7.1–7.2	138	A	1.3
103	B	2.4	139	D	1.3
104	D	2.4	140	C	1.3

Question	Answer	Objective	Question	Answer	Objective
141	A	1.3	177	B	1.1–1.3
142	B	1.3	178	A	1.1–1.3
143	C	1.3	179	C	1.1
144	B	1.3	180	B	1.1
145	D	1.3	181	A	1.1
146	A	1.3	182	C	1.1
147	B	1.3	183	B	1.1
148	A	1.3	184	D	1.1
149	D	1.3	185	C	1.1
150	C	1.3	186	B	1.1
151	A	1.3	187	C	1.1
152	C	1.3	188	A	1.1
153	B	1.3	189	D	1.1
154	D	1.3	190	C	1.1
155	A	8.1	191	B	1.1
156	D	8.1	192	D	1.1
157	B	8.1	193	C	1.1
158	C	8.1	194	B	1.1
159	D	2.3	195	A	6.3
160	C	3.3	196	B	6.3
161	B	3.3	197	C	6.3
162	A	3.3	198	D	6.3
163	D	2.2	199	C	1.4
164	A	2.2	200	A	4.1
165	B	2.2	201	D	4.1
166	C	2.2	202	B	4.1
167	A	2.2	203	A	4.1
168	B	2.2	204	B	4.1
169	C	2.2	205	C	4.1
170	D	2.2	206	D	4.1
171	B	2.2	207	B	3.3
172	D	2.2	208	C	3.3
173	A	2.2	209	D	3.3
174	C	2.2	210	A	3.3
175	D	1.1–1.3	211	C	3.2
176	C	1.1–1.3	212	A	3.2

Question	Answer	Objective	Question	Answer	Objective
213	B	2.1	249	B	3.1
214	D	2.1	250	D	3.2–3.3
215	A	2.1	251	B	6.1–6.3
216	D	2.1	252	D	6.1–6.3
217	B	2.1	253	C	6.1–6.3
218	C	2.1	254	A	6.1–6.3
219	D	6.1–6.3	255	D	6.1–6.3
220	C	4.1	256	A	6.1–6.3
221	A	4.1	257	C	6.1–6.3
222	B	4.1	258	B	6.1–6.3
223	C	5.1	259	A	6.1–6.3
224	B	5.1	260	B	6.1–6.3
225	D	5.1	261	D	3.4
226	A	5.1	262	C	6.1–6.3
227	B	4.1	263	D	6.1–6.3
228	A	4.1	264	A	6.1–6.3
229	C	5.1	265	C	6.1–6.3
230	D	5.1	266	B	6.1–6.3
231	A	5.1	267	A	5.1
232	D	3.2	268	B	5.1
233	B	3.2	269	C	5.1
234	C	3.2	270	D	5.1
235	D	2.3	271	B	5.1
236	A	2.3	272	D	5.1
237	C	2.3	273	C	5.1
238	B	2.3	274	A	5.1
239	C	5.1	275	D	5.1
240	A	5.1	276	A	5.1
241	B	5.1	277	C	5.1
242	D	5.1	278	B	5.1
243	A	1.3	279	A	5.1
244	D	1.3	280	D	6.1
245	B	3.2	281	B	5.1
246	C	3.2	282	C	5.1
247	A	3.1	283	D	5.1
248	C	3.1	284	C	5.1

1

Question	Answer	Objective	Question	Answer	Objective
285	B	5.1	321	D	6.1–6.2
286	A	5.1	322	B	6.1–6.2
287	C	5.1	323	A	2.4
288	A	5.1	324	C	2.4
289	B	5.1	325	B	2.4
290	D	5.1	326	C	2.4
291	C	5.1	327	A	2.4
292	D	5.1	328	D	2.4
293	B	5.1	329	C	7.1
294	A	5.1	330	D	7.1
295	D	5.2	331	A	7.1
296	A	4.1	332	B	5.1
297	C	4.1	333	D	5.1
298	B	4.1	334	B	5.1
299	A	4.1	335	A	7.1–7.2
300	D	6.1	336	C	7.1–7.2
301	B	6.1	337	B	7.1–7.2
302	C	6.1	338	C	4.1
303	B	6.1	339	A	4.1
304	A	5.1–5.3	340	D	4.1
305	C	5.1–5.3	341	A	4.1
306	D	5.1–5.3	342	B	4.1
307	A	5.1	343	D	4.1
308	B	5.1	344	C	4.1
309	D	5.1	345	B	4.1
310	B	5.1	346	C	4.2
311	A	6.1	347	A	4.2
312	C	6.1	348	D	4.2
313	B	6.1–6.3	349	A	4.2
314	C	6.1–6.3	350	C	4.2
315	D	6.1–6.3	351	D	4.2
316	A	6.1–6.3	352	B	4.2
317	C	6.1–6.2	353	C	8.1–8.2
318	D	6.1–6.2	354	B	8.1–8.2
319	A	6.1–6.2	355	D	8.1–8.2
320	B	6.1–6.2	356	A	8.1–8.2

Question	Answer	Objective
357	B	8.1–8.2
358	A	8.1–8.2
359	D	8.1–8.2
360	C	8.1–8.2
361	A	8.1–8.2
362	C	8.1–8.2
363	D	8.1–8.2
364	B	8.1–8.2
365	C	8.1–8.2
366	B	8.1–8.2
367	D	7.1
368	A	7.1

Question	Answer	Objective
369	B	7.1
370	A	7.1
371	D	7.1–7.2
372	C	7.1–7.2
373	A	7.1–7.2
374	C	7.1–7.2
375	D	7.3
376	B	7.3
377	C	7.2
378	B	7.2
379	D	7.2

CompTIA A+ 220-602

QUESTION 1

You can use the following command to get a Command Prompt window in Windows XP:

A. Run
B. Cmd
C. Start
D. Prompt

EXPLANATION

In Windows XP, you can enter the command Cmd in the Run dialog box to get a Command Prompt window.

QUESTION 2

The FAT file system is named after the:

A. File allocation table
B. Tracks list
C. Sectors map
D. Clusters list

EXPLANATION

The FAT file system is named after the file allocation table (FAT).

QUESTION 3

The following term describes a list of subdirectories and files:

A. Sector table
B. Directory table
C. Track table
D. Cluster table

EXPLANATION

A directory table is a list of subdirectories and files.

QUESTION 4

What type of partition can support only one logical drive?
  A. Primary
  B. Multiple
  C. Extended
  D. Logical

EXPLANATION

A primary partition can have only one logical drive.

QUESTION 5

You can use the following tool in Windows XP/2000 to manage partitions and logical drives:
  A. Disk Management
  B. Control Panel
  C. Windows Explorer
  D. Disk Connections

EXPLANATION

After Windows 2000/XP is installed, you can use the Disk Management tool to view partitions, create new ones, and format logical drives.

QUESTION 6

Windows 9x/Me supported the following type of applications:
  A. Solaris
  B. Unix
  C. Mac OS
  D. DOS or Windows 3.x

EXPLANATION

Windows 9x/Me was written to work with DOS or Windows 3.x applications, which was an early selling point for Windows 9x/Me

QUESTION 7

What are the most useful tools to explore files and folders on a Windows-based computer?
  A. Control Panel and taskbar
  B. System tray and taskbar
  C. Control Panel and system tray
  D. My Computer and Windows Explorer

2

EXPLANATION

The two most useful tools to explore files and folders on your computer are My Computer and Windows Explorer.

QUESTION 8

What is the easiest way to manage drives, disks, folders, and files in Explorer or My Computer?

A. Use the shortcut menus
B. Use the system tray
C. Use the taskbar
D. Use the Control Panel

EXPLANATION

The easiest way to manage drives, disks, folders, and files in Explorer or My Computer is to use the shortcut menus.

QUESTION 9

To create a file for Windows 2000/XP, right-click in the unused white area in the right window of Explorer and select the following option from the shortcut menu:

A. Arrange Icons
B. Properties
C. New
D. Options

EXPLANATION

To create a file for Windows 2000/XP, right-click in the unused white area in the right window of Explorer and select New from the shortcut menu.

QUESTION 10

The following term refers to the folder that contains a child folder:

A. Down folder
B. Parent folder
C. Bigger folder
D. System folder

EXPLANATION

A parent folder is the folder that contains the child folder.

QUESTION 11

You can delete a folder from Explorer using the following option from the shortcut menu:

A. New
B. Options
C. Delete
D. Properties

EXPLANATION

To delete a folder from Explorer, right-click the folder and select Delete from the shortcut menu.

QUESTION 12

In Windows XP, the properties assigned to a file are called:

A. File options
B. File attributes
C. File icons
D. File bin

EXPLANATION

Using Explorer or My Computer, you can view and change the properties assigned to a file; these properties are called the file attributes.

QUESTION 13

In Windows 2000/XP, the following file attribute is used to determine if a file has changed since the last backup:

A. Archive
B. Read-only
C. Change
D. Hidden

EXPLANATION

The archive attribute is used to determine if a file has changed since the last backup.

QUESTION 14

The following file attribute can be changed with the Attrib command, but not by using Explorer:

A. Hidden attribute
B. Archive attribute
C. Change attribute
D. System attribute

2

EXPLANATION

The system attribute can be changed with the Attrib command, but not by using Explorer.

QUESTION 15

What is the primary Windows tool to solve hardware problems?
 A. Device Manager
 B. Control Panel
 C. System Properties
 D. Shortcut menu

EXPLANATION

Device Manager is your primary Windows tool when solving problems with hardware.

QUESTION 16

The following Windows tool allows you to make changes, update drivers, and uninstall device drivers:
 A. Control Panel
 B. System tray
 C. Device Manager
 D. Taskbar

EXPLANATION

Using Device Manager, you can make changes, update drivers, and uninstall device drivers.

QUESTION 17

In Windows XP, you can enter the following command in the Run dialog box to open the Device Manager:
 A. Device.cpl
 B. Manager.dev
 C. Manager.cpl
 D. Devmgmt.msc

EXPLANATION

To access Device Manager under Windows XP, you can enter Devmgmt.msc in the Run dialog box.

QUESTION 18

To uninstall a device using the Windows Device Manager, select the following option from the shortcut menu:

A. Rollback
B. Uninstall
C. Change device
D. Fix device

EXPLANATION

One thing you can do if you have a problem with an installed device is to use Device Manager to uninstall the device. Right-click the device and click Uninstall on the shortcut menu.

QUESTION 19

In Device Manager, the following symbol indicates a disabled device:

A. Exclamation point
B. Blue I
C. Red X
D. Green question mark

EXPLANATION

In Device Manager, a red X through the device name indicates a disabled device.

QUESTION 20

In Device Manager, the following symbol indicates that automatic settings were not used and resources have been manually assigned:

A. Exclamation point
B. Blue I
C. Green question mark
D. Red X

EXPLANATION

In Device Manager, a blue I on a white field indicates that automatic settings were not used and resources have been manually assigned.

2

QUESTION 21

The following can be used to boot a system and repair or reinstall the Windows operating system:

A. Virus detection software
B. Disk partition software
C. Spyware software
D. Recovery CD

EXPLANATION

A recovery CD can be used to boot a system and repair or reinstall the Windows operating system.

QUESTION 22

If you have a notebook computer or a brand-name computer, you should use the following to recover your system:

A. Recovery CD provided by the manufacturer
B. Windows Setup CD
C. Off-the-shell Windows Setup CD
D. Windows XP Home Edition Setup CD

EXPLANATION

If you have a notebook computer or a brand-name computer such as a Dell, IBM, or Gateway, use the recovery CD provided by the manufacturer instead of a regular Windows Setup CD.

QUESTION 23

The following can be used to test a serial, parallel, USB, network, or other port:

A. Ground plug tester
B. Network cable tester
C. AC outlet ground tester
D. Loop-back plug

EXPLANATION

A loop-back plug is used to test a serial, parallel, USB, network, or other port.

QUESTION 24

The following explains how to properly handle substances such as chemical solvents:
  A. Optifix
  B. Material safety data sheet (MSDS)
  C. Head cleaner sheet
  D. Cleaner mat

EXPLANATION

A material safety data sheet (MSDS) explains how to properly handle substances such as chemical solvents.

QUESTION 25

The following tool monitors the boot process and reports errors, usually as coded numbers on a small LED panel:
  A. POST diagnostic card
  B. Chip extractor card
  C. BIOS LED card
  D. Recovery card

EXPLANATION

A POST diagnostic card monitors the boot process and reports errors, usually as coded numbers on a small LED panel on the card.

QUESTION 26

The following plan helps you to manage failures when they occur:
  A. Preventive maintenance plan
  B. Regular maintenance plan
  C. Disaster recovery plan
  D. PC maintenance plan

EXPLANATION

You need a disaster recovery plan to manage failures when they occur.

QUESTION 27

The following is the firewall that comes with Windows XP:
  A. Norton Internet Security
  B. Windows Firewall
  C. McAfee Internet Suite
  D. ZoneAlarm Pro

EXPLANATION

For Windows XP, you can use Windows Firewall. (Windows 2000 and Windows 9x/Me do not offer a firewall. For these OSs, you need to use third-party software.)

QUESTION 28

You must configure your antivirus software to scan one of the following items:

A. Expansion cards
B. POST diagnostic card
C. Record book
D. E-mail attachments

EXPLANATION

Set the antivirus software to automatically scan e-mail attachments.

QUESTION 29

Microsoft continually releases new patches, fixes, and updates for the following OS:

A. Windows 95
B. Windows 3.11
C. Windows XP
D. Windows Me

EXPLANATION

Microsoft is continually releasing new patches, fixes, and updates for Windows XP.

QUESTION 30

The following Microsoft OS offers a way to automatically download and install updates:

A. Windows XP
B. Windows 2000
C. Windows Me
D. Windows 98

EXPLANATION

Windows XP offers a way to automatically download and install updates. Windows 2000 does not offer automatic updates.

QUESTION 31

The following option can keep boot viruses at bay:
  A. Keep magnets away from your computer
  B. Keep humidity levels low
  C. Block air vents on the front and rear of the computer case
  D. Disable the ability to write to the boot sector of the hard drive

EXPLANATION

In CMOS setup, disable the ability to write to the boot sector of the hard drive. This alone can keep boot viruses at bay.

QUESTION 32

Which of the following is true?
  A. High humidity can be dangerous for hard drives
  B. Blocking air vents on the front and rear of the computer case will not damage your computer
  C. Leaving the PC turned off for weeks or months could not affect your computer
  D. Because most computers are shielded, it is acceptable to keep magnets close to your computer

EXPLANATION

High humidity can be dangerous for hard drives.

QUESTION 33

How often should you delete temporary files and empty the Recycle Bin?
  A. Daily
  B. Weekly
  C. Monthly
  D. Yearly

EXPLANATION

Delete temporary files and empty the Recycle Bin monthly.

QUESTION 34

How often should you clean your keyboard?
  A. Weekly
  B. Monthly
  C. Yearly
  D. Every five years

EXPLANATION

Clean your keyboard at least once a month.

QUESTION 35

One of the following options can cause PC parts to overheat:
  A. Cool air
  B. Humidity
  C. Dust
  D. Air conditioner

EXPLANATION

Dust is not good for a PC because it insulates PC parts like a blanket, which can cause them to overheat.

QUESTION 36

The following is an important part of preventive maintenance:
  A. Ridding the PC of dust
  B. Keeping the humidity level high
  C. Keeping the room temperature high
  D. Shaking the computer case to get rid of bits of paper

EXPLANATION

Ridding the PC of dust is an important part of preventive maintenance.

QUESTION 37

Some PC technicians don't like to use a vacuum inside a PC because it can produce the following:
  A. Humidity
  B. ESD
  C. Heat
  D. Dust

EXPLANATION

Some PC technicians don't like to use a vacuum inside a PC because they're concerned that the vacuum might produce ESD.

QUESTION 38

The following can be used instead of an antistatic vacuum to clean inside the PC case:

A. Water
B. Monitor cleaner
C. Optifix
D. Compressed air

EXPLANATION

If you don't have an antistatic vacuum, you can use compressed air to blow the dust out of the chassis, power supply, and fans.

QUESTION 39

You should dispose of laser printer toner cartridges in the following way:

A. Return them to the manufacturer or dealer
B. Dispose of them in the regular trash
C. Burn them
D. Bury them

EXPLANATION

To dispose of laser printer toner cartridges, return them to the manufacturer or dealer to be recycled.

QUESTION 40

The following is true when disposing of a monitor:

A. Always dispose of a charged monitor
B. Do physical damage to the device before disposing of it
C. Burn it before disposing of it
D. Discharge it before disposing of it

EXPLANATION

Discharge a monitor before disposing of it.

QUESTION 41

The following is true when disposing of storage media:

A. Do not dispose of it with your regular trash
B. Bury it
C. Do physical damage to the device before disposing of it
D. Discharge it before disposing of it

EXPLANATION

When disposing of storage media, do physical damage to the device so it is not possible for sensitive data to be stolen.

QUESTION 42

Most CRT monitors today are designed to discharge if they are allowed to sit unplugged for:

A. Less than 30 minutes

B. 60 minutes or more

C. 2 hours or more

D. One day

EXPLANATION

Most CRT monitors today are designed to discharge if they are allowed to sit unplugged for 60 minutes or more.

QUESTION 43

The following term describes an electrical charge at rest:

A. DIP discharge

B. Hertz discharge

C. dB discharge

D. Electrostatic discharge

EXPLANATION

Electrostatic discharge (ESD), commonly known as static electricity, is an electrical charge at rest.

QUESTION 44

If you can hear the static charge, you discharged at least the following amount of volts of static electricity:

A. 1,500

B. 3,000

C. 6,000

D. 10,000

EXPLANATION

If you hear the discharge, you released at least 6,000 volts.

QUESTION 45

Static shielding bags are a type of the following:
- A. ESD bracelet
- B. Ground bracelet
- C. Ground mat
- D. Faraday Cage

EXPLANATION

These bags are a type of Faraday Cage, named after Michael Faraday, who built the first cage in 1836.

QUESTION 46

The following is true when fixing a computer problem:
- A. Leave important data on the disk without being backed up
- B. It is not your job to back up the user's data before working on the PC
- C. Back up any important data as soon as possible
- D. Blame the user for not backing up the data

EXPLANATION

Be sure to back up any important data that is not currently backed up before you begin work on the PC.

QUESTION 47

The following is true when solving a PC problem:
- A. Don't ask users questions about the problem
- B. Always start by turning the computer off
- C. Always start by turning the computer on
- D. Find out what works and doesn't work before you take anything apart

EXPLANATION

Find out what works and doesn't work before you take anything apart or try some possible fix.

QUESTION 48

The following is true when fixing a computer problem:
- A. Approach the problem systematically
- B. Make assumptions
- C. Don't ask users questions about the problem
- D. Don't back up data that is not already backed up

EXPLANATION

When trying to solve the problem, start at the beginning and walk through the situation in a thorough, careful way. This one rule is invaluable.

QUESTION 49

The following is true when solving a PC problem:
  A. Analyze the problem, and don't make an initial determination
  B. Make assumptions
  C. Always start by turning the computer on
  D. Check simple things first

EXPLANATION

Most problems are so simple that we overlook them because we expect the problem to be difficult. Don't let the complexity of computers fool you. Most problems are easy to fix.

QUESTION 50

The following is true when fixing a computer problem:
  A. Make assumptions about the problem
  B. Trade known good for suspected bad
  C. Ignore user comments about the problem
  D. Check simple things last

EXPLANATION

Trade known good for suspected bad. When diagnosing hardware problems, this method works well if you can draw from a group of parts that you know work correctly.

QUESTION 51

The following means that the BIOS has successfully completed POST:
  A. Hear continuous beeps
  B. Hear one beep followed by two, three, or four beeps
  C. Hear two beeps followed by four beeps
  D. Hear one beep during the boot and see a blank screen

EXPLANATION

If you hear one beep during the boot and you see a blank screen, then BIOS has successfully completed POST, which includes a test of the video card.

QUESTION 52

The following tool protects equipment against sudden changes in power level, such as spikes from lightning strikes:

A. Spike tester
B. AC outlet ground tester
C. Surge suppressor
D. UL filter

EXPLANATION

A surge suppressor, also called a surge protector, protects equipment against sudden changes in power level, such as spikes from lightning strikes.

QUESTION 53

The following unit measures the work or energy required to produce one watt of power in one second:

A. Joule
B. Volt
C. Hertz
D. Amp

EXPLANATION

One joule (pronounced "jewel") is the work or energy required to produce one watt of power in one second.

QUESTION 54

The following term describes the voltage point at which a suppressor begins to absorb or block voltage:

A. Joule
B. Clamping voltage
C. Amp
D. Hertz

EXPLANATION

Clamping voltage (also called let-through voltage) is the voltage point at which a suppressor begins to absorb or block voltage.

QUESTION 55

The following tool regulates, or conditions, the power, providing continuous voltage during brownouts:

A. Power conditioner
B. Surge protector
C. Surge suppressor
D. Brown filter

EXPLANATION

In addition to providing protection against spikes, power conditioners also regulate, or condition, the power, providing continuous voltage during brownouts.

QUESTION 56

The following term describes temporary voltage reductions:

A. Swells
B. Sags
C. Spikes
D. Amps

EXPLANATION

Brownouts or sags are temporary voltage reductions.

QUESTION 57

The following term describes a UPS device that uses a battery-powered circuit when AC input fails:

A. Inline device
B. Online device
C. Line-interactive device
D. Standby device

EXPLANATION

In a standby UPS device, a battery-powered circuit is used when AC input fails.

QUESTION 58

The following type of UPS combines the features of a standby UPS and an inline device:

A. Online
B. Static
C. Line-interactive
D. Battery-powered

EXPLANATION

A line-interactive UPS device combines the features of a standby UPS and an inline UPS.

QUESTION 59

The following type of UPS can be controlled by software from a computer:
  A. Smart UPS
  B. Line-interactive
  C. Standby
  D. Online

EXPLANATION

A smart UPS (also called an intelligent UPS) can be controlled by software from a computer.

QUESTION 60

The following is true when buying a UPS:
  A. Buy a UPS that runs at full capacity
  B. Do not buy a UPS that runs at full capacity
  C. Always buy a smart UPS
  D. An intelligent UPS is not suitable for a Web server

EXPLANATION

When you purchase a UPS, do not buy a UPS that runs at full capacity.

QUESTION 61

The following item might solve the problem of intermittent errors caused by noise in the power line to the PC:
  A. Grounded bracelet
  B. Grounded mat
  C. Line conditioner
  D. AC outlet power tester

EXPLANATION

A line conditioner might solve the problem of intermittent errors caused by noise in the power line to the PC.

QUESTION 62

The following is a symptom of an intermittent problem with the electrical system:
- A. You can't turn your computer on (it looks dead)
- B. You can't turn your computer off
- C. The environment is very humid
- D. The power supply overheats and becomes hot to the touch

EXPLANATION

The power supply overheating and becoming hot to the touch might indicate an intermittent electrical problem.

QUESTION 63

What is the standard power supply of a system?
- A. 160 watts
- B. About 250 watts
- C. 450 watts
- D. More than 500 watts

EXPLANATION

A system with a standard power supply of about 250 watts that has multiple hard drives, multiple CD drives, and several expansion cards is most likely operating above the rated capacity of the power supply.

QUESTION 64

The following is true about computers:
- A. You can operate your PC even if the power supply fan does not work
- B. Cooling fans in computers are really not necessary
- C. Don't operate the PC if the power supply fan does not work
- D. An improperly working fan will never cause power supply problems

EXPLANATION

Don't operate the PC if the fan does not work. Computers without cooling fans can quickly overheat and damage chips.

QUESTION 65

What is the easiest way to fix a power supply?
- A. Replace it
- B. Open it and fix it
- C. Let it cool down for about 10 minutes
- D. Increase the humidity level inside the case

EXPLANATION

The easiest way to fix a power supply that you suspect is faulty is to replace it.

QUESTION 66

What unit is used to measure the processor core frequency?
- A. Watts
- B. Volts
- C. Amps
- D. Gigahertz

EXPLANATION

Processor core frequency is measured in gigahertz, such as 3.2 GHz.

QUESTION 67

The following term refers to the number of bits a processor can process at one time:
- A. Bus width
- B. Word size
- C. Bus speed
- D. Cache speed

EXPLANATION

Word size, either 32 bits or 64 bits, is the number of bits a processor can process at one time.

QUESTION 68

The following term refers to the processor chip:
- A. CMOS
- B. BIOS
- C. POST
- D. Die

EXPLANATION

Today's processors all have some memory on the processor chip (called a die).

QUESTION 69

What is Intel's maximum temperature limit for the processor?
- A. 185 degrees F
- B. 250 degrees F
- C. 300 degrees F
- D. 310 degrees F

EXPLANATION

Because a processor generates so much heat, computer systems use a cooling assembly to keep temperatures below the Intel maximum limit of 185 degrees Fahrenheit/ 85 degrees Celsius.

QUESTION 70

Good processor cooling fans maintain a temperature in the following range:

A. 60-70 degrees F
B. 90-110 degrees F
C. 100-150 degrees F
D. 120-140 degrees F

EXPLANATION

Good processor cooling fans maintain a temperature of 90–110 degrees F (32–43 degrees C).

QUESTION 71

The following term refers to a clip-on device that mounts on top of the processor; fingers or fins at its base pull the heat away from the processor:

A. BTX
B. Thermaltake
C. Heat sink
D. Cooler

EXPLANATION

A heat sink is a clip-on device that mounts on top of the processor; fingers or fins at its base pull the heat away from the processor.

QUESTION 72

The following term is sometimes used to refer to the combination heat sink and cooling fan:

A. Thermaltake
B. Cooler
C. BTX
D. Parallel fan

EXPLANATION

The combination heat sink and cooling fan is sometimes called a cooler.

QUESTION 73

The following term refers to a heat sink carrying an electrical charge that causes it to act as an electrical thermal transfer device:

A. Cooling fan
B. Cooler
C. Thermaltake
D. Peltier

EXPLANATION

A peltier is a heat sink carrying an electrical charge that causes it to act as an electrical thermal transfer device.

QUESTION 74

What is the most popular method of cooling overclocked processors?

A. Water cooler unit
B. Power supply fan
C. Grounded fan
D. Peltier

EXPLANATION

The most popular method of cooling overclocked processors is a water cooler unit.

QUESTION 75

The following tool might be installed on the motherboard to control the amount of voltage to the processor:

A. Socket 370
B. Voltage regulator module (VRM)
C. Heat sink
D. Cooler

EXPLANATION

The motherboard might use a voltage regulator module (VRM) installed on the board to control the amount of voltage to the processor.

QUESTION 76

What is the first step in preparing the motherboard to go in the case?

A. Set the jumpers
B. Set the spacers
C. Set the CPU frequency multiplier
D. Set the case power supply

2

EXPLANATION

The first step in preparing the motherboard to go in the case is to set the jumpers or DIP switches.

QUESTION 77

The following type of device is an input device that inputs biological data about a person:
   A. Touch screen
   B. Optical mouse
   C. Biometric device
   D. Touch pad

EXPLANATION

A biometric device is an input device that inputs biological data about a person.

QUESTION 78

What is the biggest disadvantage to using biometric devices?
   A. The danger of false negatives or false positives
   B. They are very expensive
   C. They are very bulky
   D. They weigh too much

EXPLANATION

The biggest disadvantage to using biometric devices is the danger of false negatives or false positives.

QUESTION 79

LCD monitors are also called:
   A. Flat panel monitors
   B. CRT monitors
   C. TV monitors
   D. Box monitors

EXPLANATION

LCD monitors are also called flat panel monitors for the desktop.

QUESTION 80

Many monitors use the following technology, in which the filaments at the back of the cathode tube shoot a beam of electrons to the screen at the front of the tube:

A. LCD
B. Plasma
C. Liquid gel
D. CRT

EXPLANATION

Many monitors use CRT technology, in which the filaments at the back of the cathode tube shoot a beam of electrons to the screen at the front of the tube.

QUESTION 81

The following type of monitor produces an image using a liquid crystal material made of large, easily polarized molecules:

A. Liquid gel
B. LCD
C. CRT
D. Cathode-ray

EXPLANATION

An LCD monitor produces an image using a liquid crystal material made of large, easily polarized molecules.

QUESTION 82

TFT display is sometimes called:

A. Passive matrix display
B. Cathode-ray display
C. Active matrix display
D. Tubular display

EXPLANATION

TFT display is sometimes called active matrix display.

QUESTION 83

For CRT monitors, the following term represents the number of times in one second an electronic beam can fill the screen with lines from top to bottom:

A. Refresh rate
B. Horizontal scan rate
C. Diagonal scan rate
D. Linear scan rate

EXPLANATION

For CRT monitors, the refresh rate, or vertical scan rate, is the number of times in one second an electronic beam can fill the screen with lines from top to bottom.

QUESTION 84

The following type of CRT monitors draw a screen by making two passes:
  A. LCD
  B. Noninterlaced
  C. Interlaced
  D. Triad

EXPLANATION

Interlaced CRT monitors draw a screen by making two passes.

QUESTION 85

The following term refers to the distance between the spots, or dots, on a CRT screen that the electronic beam hits:
  A. Triad
  B. Dot pitch
  C. Interlaced
  D. Noninterlaced

EXPLANATION

Dot pitch is the distance between the spots, or dots, on a CRT screen that the electronic beam hits.

QUESTION 86

For CRT monitors, the following term represents a measure of how many spots on a CRT screen are addressable by software:
  A. Triad
  B. Dot pitch
  C. Pixel
  D. Resolution

EXPLANATION

For CRT monitors, resolution is a measure of how many spots on a CRT screen are addressable by software.

QUESTION 87

The following term means that a device can be plugged into a USB port while the computer is running:

A. PCI hot

B. USB swappable

C. Hot-swapping

D. DMA change

EXPLANATION

USB allows for hot-swapping and hot-pluggable devices. These two terms mean that a device can be plugged into a USB port while the computer is running.

QUESTION 88

The following component manages the USB bus:

A. PCI slot

B. Hub

C. DMA controller

D. USB host controller

EXPLANATION

A USB host controller, which for most motherboards is included in the chipset, manages the USB bus.

QUESTION 89

How many wires does a USB cable have?

A. 3

B. 4

C. 5

D. 7

EXPLANATION

A USB cable has four wires, two for power and two for communication.

QUESTION 90

What was the first Microsoft OS to support USB?

A. Windows 95 OSR 2.1

B. Windows 98

C. Windows Me SP1

D. Windows XP SP1

EXPLANATION

Windows 95 OSR 2.1 was the first Microsoft OS to support USB, although Windows 98 offers much improved USB support.

QUESTION 91

What is the latest modem standard?

A. S.56
B. T.12
C. V.48
D. V.92

EXPLANATION

The latest modem standard is V.92, which allows for quick connect (reduces handshake time), modem on hold (allows call waiting without breaking the connection to the ISP), and improved upload speeds for large files.

QUESTION 92

What is the sampling rate used by phone companies when converting an analog signal to digital?

A. 8,000 samples every second
B. 10,000 samples every second
C. 11,000 samples every second
D. 12,000 samples every second

EXPLANATION

A sampling rate of 8,000 samples every second is used by phone companies when converting an analog signal to digital.

QUESTION 93

The following is true about PCI cards:

A. They need exclusive use of an IRQ
B. They do not need exclusive use of an IRQ
C. They cannot be managed using a PCI controller
D. The PCI controller assigns IRQs to every PCI card

EXPLANATION

A PCI card does not need exclusive use of an IRQ because the PCI controller uses interrupt levels to manage the interrupt needs of a card.

QUESTION 94

The following is true about multiple PCI cards:
   A. The startup BIOS assigns them an interrupt level
   B. The PCI controller assigns IRQs to the cards
   C. The PCI controller assigns each PCI expansion slot an interrupt level
   D. The Device Manager assigns PCI cards an interrupt level

EXPLANATION

The PCI controller assigns each PCI expansion slot an interrupt level, named level A, B, C, D, and so forth.

QUESTION 95

Chips sometimes loosen because of thermal changes; this condition is called:
   A. Chip creep
   B. Expanding
   C. Reseating
   D. Thermal syndrome

EXPLANATION

Chips sometimes loosen because of thermal changes; this condition is called chip creep.

QUESTION 96

The following is true when troubleshooting a monitor:
   A. Wrong characters are usually the result of a bad monitor
   B. Wrong characters are not related to bad ROM and RAM chips
   C. Wrong characters are usually the result of problems with the video card
   D. Wrong characters are not the result of problems with the video card

EXPLANATION

Wrong characters are usually not the result of a bad monitor but of a problem with the video card.

QUESTION 97

The following is true when troubleshooting a monitor:
   A. Monitor flicker is usually the result of problems with the video card
   B. Monitor flicker cannot be caused by poor cable connections
   C. Wrong characters are usually the result of a bad monitor
   D. Monitor flicker can be caused by poor cable connections

EXPLANATION

Monitor flicker can be caused by poor cable connections. Check that the cable connections are snug.

QUESTION 98

A CRT monitor screen is made of the following:

A. Liquid crystal

B. Leaded glass

C. Plasma

D. Magnetic gel

EXPLANATION

A CRT monitor screen is made of leaded glass, and a monitor contains capacitors that can hold a charge even after the monitor is unplugged.

QUESTION 99

What is the file system used by a DVD?

A. NTFS

B. AFS

C. UDF

D. NFS

EXPLANATION

A DVD uses the Universal Disk Format (UDF) file system.

QUESTION 100

The following term refers to the height from which the manufacturer says you can drop a drive without making it unusable:

A. Half-life

B. Drop height

C. Crash height

D. Crash level

EXPLANATION

The drop height is the height from which the manufacturer says you can drop a drive without making it unusable.

QUESTION 101

The following term describes a group of networked computers that share a centralized directory database of user account information and security for the entire group of computers:

A. Workgroup
B. Peer-to-peer
C. Client/Server
D. Windows domain

EXPLANATION

A Windows domain is a group of networked computers that share a centralized directory database of user account information and security for the entire group of computers.

QUESTION 102

A domain uses the following networking model:

A. Client/server
B. Peer-to-peer
C. Workgroup
D. Workstations

EXPLANATION

A domain uses a client/server networking model.

QUESTION 103

Every Windows domain has the following component, which stores and controls a database of user accounts, group accounts, and computer accounts:

A. Domain server
B. Domain NOS
C. Domain controller
D. Domain workstation

EXPLANATION

Every domain has a domain controller, which stores and controls a database of user accounts, group accounts, and computer accounts.

2

QUESTION 104

Windows 2000 runs in the following two modes:
  A. PDC mode and BDC mode
  B. Native mode and mixed mode
  C. SAM mode and NOS mode
  D. Client mode and Server mode

EXPLANATION

Windows 2000 runs in two modes: native mode and mixed mode.

QUESTION 105

How many bytes are in a hard drive sector?
  A. 64
  B. 128
  C. 256
  D. 512

EXPLANATION

A hard drive is divided into 512-byte sectors.

QUESTION 106

The following partition is used to boot the OS:
  A. MBR partition
  B. Active partition
  C. POST partition
  D. Boot partition

EXPLANATION

The active partition is the partition on the hard drive that is used to boot the OS.

QUESTION 107

The following type of virus attacks the MBR master boot program:
  A. Boot sector virus
  B. Macros virus
  C. Scam
  D. Worm

EXPLANATION

A boot sector virus attacks the MBR master boot program.

QUESTION 108

The following partition stores the Windows 2000/XP operating system:
   A. System partition
   B. Active partition
   C. Boot partition
   D. POST partition

EXPLANATION

The boot partition stores the Windows 2000/XP operating system.

QUESTION 109

What is the name of the wasted disk space when using the FAT16 file system?
   A. Cluster
   B. Slack
   C. Waste
   D. Track

EXPLANATION

Using FAT16, the smallest cluster size is four sectors. If a file contains less than 2,048 bytes, the remaining bytes in the cluster are wasted. This wasted space is called slack.

QUESTION 110

NTFS uses the following database to hold information about files and directories and their locations on the hard drive:
   A. Master boot table (MBT)
   B. CMOS table
   C. Master file table (MFT)
   D. Boot table

EXPLANATION

NTFS uses a database called the master file table (MFT) to hold information about files and directories and their locations on the hard drive.

QUESTION 111

The following is true about file systems:
   A. NTFS is a recoverable file system
   B. FAT16 is a recoverable file system
   C. FAT24 is a recoverable file system
   D. FAT32 supports compression of individual files or folders

2

EXPLANATION

NTFS is a recoverable file system. It retains copies of its critical file system data and automatically recovers a failed file system.

QUESTION 112

The following is true about file systems:
  A. FAT has more overhead than NTFS
  B. FAT is not compatible with Windows 9x/Me
  C. FAT is a recoverable file system
  D. FAT has less overhead than NTFS

EXPLANATION

The FAT file system has less overhead than the NTFS file system and, therefore, works best for hard drives that are less than 500 MB.

QUESTION 113

The following term represents one way to replicate the drive to a new computer or to another drive on the same computer:
  A. Drive imaging
  B. Drive partition
  C. Installation copy
  D. Disk distribution

EXPLANATION

Drive imaging, sometimes called disk cloning or disk imaging, replicates the drive to a new computer or to another drive on the same computer.

QUESTION 114

After you install Windows XP, when you boot with a dual boot, the following menu automatically appears and asks you to select an operating system:
  A. Master boot menu
  B. Image menu
  C. Boot loader menu
  D. Boot table menu

EXPLANATION

After the Windows XP installation, when you boot with a dual boot, the boot loader menu automatically appears and asks you to select an operating system.

QUESTION 115

The following technology is used by Microsoft to prevent unlicensed use of its software:
A. Boot trap
B. Startup activation
C. BIOS license
D. Product activation

EXPLANATION

Product activation is a method used by Microsoft to prevent unlicensed use of its software.

QUESTION 116

The following term describes digital codes that can be used to authenticate the source of files:
A. Digital certificate
B. Digital signature
C. Timestamp
D. Digital stamp

EXPLANATION

Digital signatures are digital codes that can be used to authenticate the source of files.

QUESTION 117

The following is a graphical, user-friendly utility that you can use to create partitions and format logical drives:
A. Drive imaging
B. Disk imaging
C. Disk Management
D. Disk Desktop

EXPLANATION

Disk Management is a graphical, user-friendly utility that you can use to create partitions and format logical drives.

QUESTION 118

The following service is used by Windows XP when it encounters a problem with an application:
A. Device Manager
B. Error Reporting
C. Control Panel
D. System tray

EXPLANATION

When Windows XP encounters a problem with an application, it uses the Error Reporting service to collect information about the problem and display a message.

QUESTION 119

The following is a Windows 2000/XP tool useful for troubleshooting problems with Windows, applications, and hardware:

A. Event Viewer
B. Console
C. Script
D. Applet viewer

EXPLANATION

Event Viewer is a Windows 2000/XP tool useful for troubleshooting problems with Windows, applications, and hardware.

QUESTION 120

What does Windows 2000/XP call the files that are critical to a successful operating system load?

A. System root files
B. System boot data
C. System boot files
D. System state data

EXPLANATION

Windows 2000/XP calls the files that are critical to a successful operating system load the system state data.

QUESTION 121

Windows 2000/XP provides the following feature to protect system files from being accidentally changed or deleted:

A. Windows File Protection (WFP)
B. System state data
C. File State Protection (FSP)
D. File Lock

EXPLANATION

Windows 2000/XP provides a feature called Windows File Protection (WFP) to protect system files from being accidentally changed or deleted.

QUESTION 122

The following Windows XP tool can be set to routinely make snapshots of critical Windows system files that are necessary to load the OS:

A. Device Manager
B. Error Reporting
C. System Restore
D. System tray

EXPLANATION

System Restore can be set to routinely make snapshots of critical Windows system files that are necessary to load the OS.

QUESTION 123

When you back up the Windows XP system state, the registry is also backed up to the folder:

A. C:\backup
B. C:\Restore\State\Registry
C. %RestorePath%\Registry
D. %SystemRoot%\repair\RegBack

EXPLANATION

When you back up the system state, the registry is also backed up to the folder %SystemRoot%\repair\RegBack.

QUESTION 124

You can use the following Windows XP tool to back up the entire drive on which Windows is installed:

A. System Restore
B. Automated System Recovery (ASR)
C. System tray
D. System state data

EXPLANATION

You can use the Windows XP Automated System Recovery (ASR) tool to back up the entire drive on which Windows is installed.

QUESTION 125

The following command opens the Windows XP registry editor:

A. Regedit32.exe
B. Registry.exe
C. Regedit.exe
D. Registry32.exe

EXPLANATION

Windows XP has only a single registry editor, Regedit.exe.

QUESTION 126

The following Windows XP tool lets you view the applications and processes running on your computer as well as performance information for the processor and memory:

A. Regedit.exe
B. Task Manager
C. Device Manager
D. System Management

EXPLANATION

Task Manager (Taskman.exe) lets you view the applications and processes running on your computer as well as performance information for the processor and memory.

QUESTION 127

You can use the following Windows XP tool to find out what processes are launched at startup and to temporarily disable a process from loading:

A. System Configuration Utility
B. Task Manager
C. Regedit.exe
D. System Manager

EXPLANATION

You can use the Windows XP System Configuration Utility (Msconfig.exe), which is commonly called "M-S-config," to find out what processes are launched at startup and to temporarily disable a process from loading.

QUESTION 128

Under Windows 2000/XP, physical memory (RAM) and virtual memory are both managed by the following component:

A. System Restore

B. Services Console

C. Device Manager

D. Virtual Memory Manager

EXPLANATION

Under Windows 2000/XP, physical memory (RAM) and virtual memory (space on the hard drive) are both managed by the Virtual Memory Manager (VMM).

QUESTION 129

The following type of user account is used at the domain level, created by an administrator using Windows 2000 Server or Windows Server 2003, and stored in the SAM database on a Windows domain controller:

A. Local user account

B. Global user account

C. Built-in user account

D. Central user account

EXPLANATION

Global user accounts, sometimes called domain user accounts, are used at the domain level, created by an administrator using Windows 2000 Server or Windows Server 2003, and stored in the SAM (security accounts manager) database on a Windows domain controller.

QUESTION 130

The following type of user account is created on a local computer and allows a user access to only that one computer:

A. Central user account

B. Built-in user account

C. Global user account

D. Local user account

EXPLANATION

A local user account is created on a local computer and allows a user access to only that one computer.

QUESTION 131

The following term refers to a predefined set of permissions and rights assigned to user accounts:

A. User group
B. Built-in user account
C. Central group
D. Local user account

EXPLANATION

A user group is a predefined set of permissions and rights assigned to user accounts. It is an efficient way for an administrator to manage multiple user accounts that require these same permissions and rights.

QUESTION 132

In Windows 2000/XP, the following type of account can read from and write to parts of the system other than their own local drive, install applications, and perform limited administrative tasks:

A. Backup Operator
B. Guest
C. Power User
D. Limited User

EXPLANATION

A Power User account can read from and write to parts of the system other than their own local drive, install applications, and perform limited administrative tasks.

QUESTION 133

The following command can be used to view and change the access control for files and folders:

A. User
B. UsrGrp
C. ChgUsr
D. Cacls

EXPLANATION

The Cacls (change access control lists) command can be used to view and change the access control for files and folders.

QUESTION 134

With the following type of profiles, settings established by a user at one computer are stored in a file on a file server on the network and shared with all computers in the workgroup:

A. Group
B. Mandatory
C. Roaming user
D. Local user

EXPLANATION

With roaming user profiles, settings established by a user at one computer are stored in a file on a file server on the network and shared with all computers in the workgroup.

QUESTION 135

In Windows 2000/XP, an administrator creates group, roaming, and mandatory profiles using the following:

A. Device Manager
B. Computer Management console
C. User Management
D. Accounts console

EXPLANATION

An administrator creates group, roaming, and mandatory profiles using the Computer Management console.

QUESTION 136

What is the maximum number of characters for a Windows 2000/XP password?

A. 127
B. 150
C. 210
D. 256

EXPLANATION

Passwords can be up to 127 characters.

QUESTION 137

How can you log on using the built-in administrator account in Windows XP?

A. Using the Welcome screen
B. Pressing the Ctrl+Alt+Del keys
C. Pressing the Esc key in the Welcome screen
D. Pressing the Tab key in the Welcome screen

EXPLANATION

If you want to log onto the system using the built-in administrator account, press Ctrl+Alt+Del.

QUESTION 138

To access the Group Policy console, enter the following command in the Run dialog box:

A. policy.grp
B. editpolicy.exe
C. editplc.com
D. gpedit.msc

EXPLANATION

To access the Group Policy console, enter gpedit.msc in the Run dialog box.

QUESTION 139

The following USMT command is used to copy the information from the old computer to a server or removable media:

A. scanstate
B. loadstate
C. copyuser
D. duplicate

EXPLANATION

The scanstate command is used to copy the information from the old computer to a server or removable media.

QUESTION 140

The following USMT command is used to copy the information from a server or removable media to the new computer:

A. download
B. duplicatestate
C. loadstate
D. scanstate

EXPLANATION

The loadstate command is used to copy the information to the new computer.

QUESTION 141

The following occurs when a single file is placed in clusters that are not right next to each other:
A. Clustering
B. Fragmentation
C. Chaining
D. Grouping

EXPLANATION

Fragmentation occurs when a single file is placed in clusters that are not right next to each other.

QUESTION 142

The following term defines clusters that are pointed to by more than one chain:
A. Fragments
B. Lost clusters
C. Lost allocation units
D. Cross-linked clusters

EXPLANATION

Clusters are called cross-linked clusters when more than one chain points to them.

QUESTION 143

Using Windows 2000/XP, searching for and repairing file system errors and bad sectors can be done using the following command:
A. Rededit.exe
B. Fdisk.exe
C. Chkdsk.exe
D. FATCheck.exe

EXPLANATION

Using Windows 2000/XP, searching for and repairing file system errors and bad sectors can be done using Chkdsk.exe.

QUESTION 144

The following software works under Windows 2000/XP at the file, folder, or volume level by rewriting data in files in a mathematically coded format that uses less space:
A. Compression
B. Defragment
C. Clustering
D. Chkdsk.exe

EXPLANATION

Compression software works under Windows 2000/XP at the file, folder, or volume level by rewriting data in files in a mathematically coded format that uses less space.

QUESTION 145

The following type of repeater simply amplifies the incoming signal, noise and all:
  A. Attenuation repeater
  B. Signal-regenerating repeater
  C. Network repeater
  D. Amplifier repeater

EXPLANATION

An amplifier repeater simply amplifies the incoming signal, noise and all.

QUESTION 146

Ethernet uses the following type of repeater:
  A. Signal-regenerating repeater
  B. Attenuation repeater
  C. Amplifier repeater
  D. Frequency repeater

EXPLANATION

Ethernet uses a signal-regenerating repeater.

QUESTION 147

What is the frequency range used by 802.11b and 802.11g?
  A. 1.2 GHz
  B. 2.0 GHz
  C. 2.4 GHz
  D. 5.2 GHz

EXPLANATION

802.11g and 802.11b use a frequency range of 2.4 GHz in the radio band and have a distance range of about 100 meters.

QUESTION 148

What is the protocol suite used on the Internet?
  A. IPX/SPX
  B. TCP/IP
  C. NetBEUI
  D. NetBIOS

EXPLANATION

TCP/IP (Transmission Control Protocol/Internet Protocol) is the protocol suite used on the Internet.

QUESTION 149

The following protocol is an NWLink protocol suite designed for use with the Novell NetWare operating system:

A. IPX/SPX

B. TCP/IP

C. NetBIOS

D. NetBEUI

EXPLANATION

IPX/SPX (Internetwork Packet Exchange/Sequenced Packet Exchange) is an NWLink protocol suite designed for use with the Novell NetWare operating system.

QUESTION 150

The following solution uses a single public IP address to access the Internet on behalf of all hosts on the network using other IP addresses:

A. DHCP

B. NAT

C. CDIR

D. IPX/SPX

EXPLANATION

NAT (Network Address Translation) uses a single public IP address to access the Internet on behalf of all hosts on the network using other IP addresses.

QUESTION 151

The following term refers to a computer that can find an IP address for another computer when only the host name and domain name are known:

A. DHCP server

B. SNMP server

C. DNS server

D. ICMP server

EXPLANATION

A DNS server and a WINS server are computers that can find an IP address for another computer when only the host name and domain name are known.

QUESTION 152

The following term describes a computer or other device that allows a computer on one network to communicate with a computer on another network:

A. Host
B. Domain
C. Client
D. Gateway

EXPLANATION

A gateway is a computer or other device that allows a computer on one network to communicate with a computer on another network.

QUESTION 153

The following can be used to control which wireless adapters can use the access point:

A. Tx rate
B. MAC address filtering
C. Noise filtering
D. CDIR filtering

EXPLANATION

MAC address filtering can be used to control which wireless adapters can use the access point.

QUESTION 154

What is the downside of having a wireless network?

A. Wireless networks require expensive cabling
B. Wireless networks require expensive equipment
C. Wireless networks cannot support routers
D. Wireless networks must be properly secured

EXPLANATION

The downside of having a wireless network is that if we don't have the proper security in place, anyone with a wireless computer within range of your access point can use the network.

QUESTION 155

WPA2 encryption is also called:

A. WEP
B. WEB
C. 802.11i
D. DES

EXPLANATION

The latest and best wireless encryption standard is WPA2, also called the 802.11i standard.

QUESTION 156

What is the preferred encryption method when transmitting sensitive data over a wireless connection?
  A. VPN
  B. WPA
  C. WEP
  D. 802.11i

EXPLANATION

The encryption methods used by VPN are stronger than WEP or WPA and are the preferred method when transmitting sensitive data over a wireless connection.

QUESTION 157

What of the following security features is essential to keep others from hacking into your wireless data?
  A. Disable SSID broadcasting
  B. Use encryption
  C. Filter MAC addresses
  D. Change the default SSID

EXPLANATION

Encryption is essential to keep others from hacking into your wireless data.

QUESTION 158

In TCP/IP, the protocol that guarantees packet delivery is:
  A. TCP
  B. UDP
  C. IP
  D. ATP

EXPLANATION

In TCP/IP, the protocol that guarantees packet delivery is TCP (Transmission Control Protocol).

2

QUESTION 159

UDP is sometimes called:
   A. Connection-oriented protocol
   B. Effort-less protocol
   C. Connectionless protocol
   D. Internet Protocol

EXPLANATION

UDP is called a connectionless protocol or a best-effort protocol.

QUESTION 160

The following Windows 2000/XP tool displays information about current TCP/IP connections:
   A. FTP
   B. Ipconfig
   C. Route
   D. Netstat

EXPLANATION

Netstat displays information about current TCP/IP connections.

QUESTION 161

The following Windows 2000/XP tool traces and displays the route taken from the host to a remote destination:
   A. Tracert
   B. Route
   C. Ipconfig
   D. Nbtstat

EXPLANATION

Tracert traces and displays the route taken from the host to a remote destination.

QUESTION 162

The following network equipment can filter ports so that outside clients cannot communicate with inside services that are listening at these ports:
   A Hub
   B. Repeater
   C. Access Point
   D. Firewall

EXPLANATION

A firewall can filter ports so that outside clients cannot communicate with inside services that are listening at these ports.

QUESTION 163

What is the solution for securing private data traveling over a public network?
  A. WPA
  B. WEP
  C. VPN
  D. WPA2

EXPLANATION

The solution for securing private data traveling over a public network is a virtual private network (VPN).

QUESTION 164

To set up a VPN on the corporate side, the network administrator will most likely use the following to manage the VPN:
  A. FTP firewall
  B. VPN router
  C. Route firewall
  D. End point software

EXPLANATION

To set up a VPN on the corporate side, the network administrator will most likely use a hardware device such as a VPN router to manage the VPN.

QUESTION 165

The following term can mean HTTP over SSL or HTTP over TLS:
  A. EAP
  B. DSL
  C. SHTTP
  D. HTTPS

EXPLANATION

HTTPS (HTTP secure) can mean HTTP over SSL or HTTP over TLS.

2

QUESTION 166

The following is a code assigned to you by a certificate authority that uniquely identifies you on the Internet and includes a public key:

A. SSL

B. Digital certificate

C. HTTPS

D. Asymmetric key

EXPLANATION

A digital certificate, also called a digital ID or digital signature, is a code assigned to you by a certificate authority such as VeriSign (www.verisign.com) that uniquely identifies you on the Internet and includes a public key.

QUESTION 167

In Windows XP with Service Pack 2, the following tool tracks information about Windows Firewall, antivirus software installed and running, and automatic updates for the OS:

A. Management Console

B. Network Connections

C. Windows Security Center

D. Windows Personal Firewall

EXPLANATION

The Windows Security Center tracks information about Windows Firewall, antivirus software installed and running, and automatic updates for the OS.

QUESTION 168

The following type of battery initially provides up to 5 hours of battery life, and future versions will provide up to 10 hours of battery life:

A. DMFC

B. NiMH

C. Ni-Cad

D. AC-DC

EXPLANATION

A DMFC initially provides up to five hours of battery life, and future versions will provide up to 10 hours of battery life.

QUESTION 169

The following is true about notebook batteries:
  A. For all batteries, recharging too soon can shorten the battery life
  B. For some batteries, recharging too soon can shorten the battery life
  C. For all batteries, don't use them until they are fully recharged
  D. For all batteries, don't leave the battery in the notebook while the notebook is turned on and connected to an electrical outlet

EXPLANATION

For some notebook batteries, don't recharge the battery pack until all the power is used. Recharging too soon can shorten the battery life.

QUESTION 170

The following is true about notebooks:
  A. CD and DVD drives use a lot of power
  B. Leaving a battery in a notebook for extended periods when it is not used cannot damage the battery
  C. CD and DVD drives don't use a lot of power
  D. Never use the standby mode with a notebook

EXPLANATION

CD and DVD drives use a lot of power. Therefore, whenever possible, connect the notebook to an electrical outlet to play a movie on DVD or burn a CD.

QUESTION 171

To access the Power Management dialog box using Windows 2000/XP, open the Control Panel and double-click the following applet:
  A. Management Console
  B. Device Manager
  C. Power Options
  D. Energy Options

EXPLANATION

To access the Power Management dialog box using Windows 2000/XP, open the Control Panel and double-click the Power Options applet.

2

QUESTION 172

What is the disadvantage of using hibernation?

A. Hibernation mode consumes a lot of power
B. Hibernation can damage your notebook
C. Hibernation is not supported by Windows 2000/XP
D. With hibernation, it takes longer for the computer to go into suspend mode and resume from it

EXPLANATION

The disadvantage of using hibernation is that it takes longer for the computer to go into suspend mode and resume from it.

QUESTION 173

Using Windows 2000/XP, you can monitor and manage the following type of batteries on notebooks:

A. ACPI- and APM-enabled
B. Port battery
C. Replicator battery
D. Fuel battery

EXPLANATION

Using Windows 2000/XP, you can monitor and manage batteries on notebooks that are ACPI- and APM-enabled.

QUESTION 174

Printers that can print on both sides of the page are called:

A. FireWire printers
B. Replicator printers
C. DPI printers
D. Duplex printers

EXPLANATION

Printing on both sides of the page is called duplex printing.

QUESTION 175

The following is an example of an impact printer:

A. Laser printer
B. Dot matrix printer
C. Ink-jet printer
D. Dye sublimation

EXPLANATION

An example of an impact printer is a dot matrix printer.

QUESTION 176

In what step of the printing process for a laser printer is the drum conditioned to contain a high electrical charge?

A. Cleaning
B. Developing
C. Conditioning
D. Fusing

EXPLANATION

In the conditioning step, the drum is conditioned to contain a high electrical charge.

QUESTION 177

In a laser printer, the following mirror detects the laser beam by reflecting it to an optical fiber:

A. Scanning mirror
B. Fusing mirror
C. Developing mirror
D. Beam detect mirror

EXPLANATION

The beam detect mirror detects the laser beam by reflecting it to an optical fiber.

QUESTION 178

The following step of the printing process for a laser printer uses heat and pressure to fuse the toner to the paper:

A. Developing
B. Fusing
C. Writing
D. Conditioning

EXPLANATION

The fusing step uses heat and pressure to fuse the toner to the paper.

2

QUESTION 179

The following type of printer has a print head that moves across the width of the paper, using pins to print a matrix of dots on the page:

A. Laser printer
B. Dot matrix printer
C. Ink-jet printer
D. Dye sublimation

EXPLANATION

A dot matrix printer has a print head that moves across the width of the paper, using pins to print a matrix of dots on the page.

QUESTION 180

What is the greatest disadvantage of solid ink printers?

A. Time it takes for the print head to heat up
B. Ink consumption
C. They can only print on photo-quality paper
D. They are hard to set up and maintain

EXPLANATION

The greatest disadvantage to solid ink printing is the time it takes for the print head to heat up to begin a print job, which is about 15 minutes.

QUESTION 181

A printer connected to a computer by way of a port on the computer is called a:

A. Network printer
B. Print server
C. Local printer
D. Ethernet printer

EXPLANATION

A printer connected to a computer by way of a port on the computer is called a local printer.

QUESTION 182

For Windows XP, by default, the Printers and Faxes window shows on the following menu:

A. Start
B. Devices
C. Applications
D. System

EXPLANATION

For Windows XP, by default, the Printers and Faxes window shows on the Start menu.

QUESTION 183

The following is true when using a shared network printer:
   A. Laser printers cannot be shared on a network
   B. The remote PC does not need the printer drivers if the printer is an ink-jet printer
   C. The remote PC does not need to have the printer drivers installed
   D. The remote PC needs to have the printer drivers installed

EXPLANATION

For a remote PC to use a shared network printer, the drivers for that printer must be installed on the remote PC.

QUESTION 184

When installing a shared printer on a Windows 9x/Me PC where the host computer is also a Windows 9x/Me PC, you must first share the following folder on the host PC:
   A. \System
   B. \Windows
   C. \Program Files
   D. \System32

EXPLANATION

When installing a shared printer on a Windows 9x/Me PC where the host computer is also a Windows 9x/Me PC, you must first share the \Windows folder on the host PC.

QUESTION 185

The following is a printer language developed by Hewlett-Packard:
   A. PostScript
   B. GDI
   C. PPM
   D. PCL

EXPLANATION

For Windows 2000/XP, a printer language that competes with PostScript is PCL (Printer Control Language). PCL was developed by Hewlett-Packard.

QUESTION 186

The following term defines the ability to print and collate multiple copies of a single print job:

A. Duplexing
B. Mopier
C. Stacking
D. Spooling

EXPLANATION

Mopier is the ability to print and collate multiple copies of a single print job.

QUESTION 187

The maintenance plan for the HP Color LaserJet 4600 printer says to replace the transfer roller assembly after printing the following number of pages:

A. 50,000
B. 65,000
C. 120,000
D. 150,000

EXPLANATION

The maintenance plan for the HP Color LaserJet 4600 printer says to replace the transfer roller assembly after printing 120,000 pages.

QUESTION 188

The following is true about cleaning a printer's outside:

A. Don't use ammonia-based cleaners
B. Use a dry cloth
C. Use ammonia-based cleaners
D. Use an antistatic vacuum cleaner to pick up stray toner

EXPLANATION

Clean the outside of the printer with a damp cloth. Don't use ammonia-based cleaners.

QUESTION 189

The following is true when cleaning a laser printer:

A. Wipe the rollers from side to side with a wet cloth
B. Do not clean the rollers
C. Do not touch the transfer roller
D. Clean the transfer roller using ammonia-based cleaners

EXPLANATION

Don't touch the soft black roller (the transfer roller), or you might affect the print quality.

QUESTION 190

To prevent the ink-jet nozzles from drying out, don't leave the ink cartridges out of their cradle for longer than:

  A. 5 minutes

  B. 15 minutes

  C. 20 minutes

  D. 30 minutes

EXPLANATION

To prevent the ink-jet nozzles from drying out, don't leave the ink cartridges out of their cradle for longer than 30 minutes.

QUESTION 191

The following is true when installing USB scanners or other scanners that are hot-pluggable:

  A. Most likely you will have to run the setup CD before connecting the scanner

  B. You must connect the scanner before using the setup CD

  C. You do not need a setup CD

  D. You cannot use hot-pluggable scanners with Windows XP SP1

EXPLANATION

For USB scanners or other scanners that are hot-pluggable, most likely you'll be told to run the setup CD before connecting the scanner.

QUESTION 192

The following is true about maintaining a scanner:

  A. You cannot adjust the scanner settings using software

  B. For most scanners, you can adjust their settings using software

  C. You must adjust scanner settings using a scanner maintenance kit

  D. You cannot adjust all HP scanner settings using software

EXPLANATION

Most scanners come bundled with utility software that you can use to adjust scanner settings.

QUESTION 193

The following is true when cleaning the glass window for a flat-bed scanner:
   A. Do not turn off the scanner
   B. Do not unplug the scanner
   C. Use isopropyl alcohol
   D. First unplug the scanner

EXPLANATION

For flat-bed scanners, you can clean the glass window with a soft dry cloth or use mild glass cleaner. First unplug the scanner.

QUESTION 194

What is the first step when troubleshooting printers and scanners?
   A. Check the network
   B. Interview the user
   C. Go to the manufacturer's Web site
   D. Unplug the device

EXPLANATION

As with all computer problems, begin troubleshooting by interviewing the user, finding out what works and doesn't work, and making an initial determination of the problem.

QUESTION 195

The following information is generally included in a printer test page:
   A. Printer memory
   B. OS version
   C. IP address
   D. Amount of toner left in cartridge

EXPLANATION

A printer test page generally prints some text, some graphics, and some information about the printer, such as the printer resolution and how much memory is installed.

QUESTION 196

The following device can be used to share one printer between two computers:
   A. Repeater
   B. Terminal
   C. T-switch
   D. Print strap

EXPLANATION

A business might use an older switch box (sometimes called a T-switch) to share one printer between two computers.

QUESTION 197

A printer's parallel cable should be compliant with the following standard:
  A. IEEE 1284
  B. IEEE 1394
  C. ANSI 203
  D. ISO 2004

EXPLANATION

A printer's parallel cable should be IEEE 1284-compliant.

QUESTION 198

The following condition can cause the toner to clump in the cartridge and give a Toner Low message:
  A. Low humidity
  B. Extreme sunlight
  C. Sunlight
  D. Extreme humidity

EXPLANATION

Extreme humidity can cause the toner to clump in the cartridge and give a Toner Low message.

QUESTION 199

When should the "warming up" message on the front panel of the printer turn off?
  A. After the network cable is connected
  B. Before establishing communication with the network
  C. As soon as the printer establishes communication with the PC
  D. Before the printer establishes communication with the PC

EXPLANATION

The "warming up" message on the front panel of the printer should turn off as soon as the printer establishes communication with the PC.

2

QUESTION 200

What is the problem if loose toner comes out with your printout?
   A. The transfer roller needs to be replaced
   B. The fuser is not reaching the proper temperature
   C. The scanning mirror needs to be cleaned
   D. The beam detector mirror needs to be replaced

EXPLANATION

If loose toner comes out with your printout, the fuser is not reaching the proper temperature.

QUESTION 201

The following is true about ink-jet printers:
   A. Use less than 20-LB paper in ink-jet printers
   B. Quality of paper does not affect the final print quality
   C. Use less than 10-LB paper in ink-jet printers
   D. Quality of paper affects the final print quality

EXPLANATION

The quality of paper determines the final print quality, especially with ink-jet printers.

QUESTION 202

The following are symptoms of a dried-out ink nozzle:
   A. Frequent paper jams
   B. Missing lines or dots on the printed page
   C. Printer heads move loosely or do not move at all
   D. Streaks or lines on the printed page

EXPLANATION

The ink nozzles on an ink-jet cartridge occasionally dry out, especially when the printer sits unused for a long time. Symptoms are missing lines or dots on the printed page.

QUESTION 203

What is the first thing you should check if a dot matrix printer print quality is poor?
   A. Printer cable
   B. Printer power cable
   C. Ribbon
   D. Printer head

EXPLANATION

Begin with the ribbon. Does it advance normally while the carriage moves back and forth? If not, replace the ribbon.

QUESTION 204

The following is true when troubleshooting scanners:
  A. Many scanners have a repair utility and troubleshooting software
  B. Parallel port scanners cannot be troubleshot
  C. You need a T-switch to troubleshoot a scanner
  D. Flat-bed scanners cannot be troubleshot

EXPLANATION

Many scanners have a repair utility and troubleshooting software that installs when the setup program runs.

QUESTION 205

What is one of the most important ways to achieve customer satisfaction?
  A. Have an expensive rate for your service
  B. Be prepared
  C. Try to solve the problem without asking for help
  D. Always recommend on-site visits

EXPLANATION

One of the most important ways to achieve customer satisfaction is to do your best by being prepared, both technically and non-technically.

QUESTION 206

The following trait distinguishes one competent technician from another in the eyes of the customer:
  A. Owning the problem
  B. Being problem-focused
  C. Treating your customers like peers
  D. Performing your work in a casual manner

EXPLANATION

Taking ownership of the customer's problem builds trust and loyalty because the customer knows you can be counted on.

2

QUESTION 207

The following trait distinguishes one competent technician from another in the eyes of the customer:
  A. Always using techie language with your customers
  B. Keeping your company's interests first
  C. Maintaining integrity and honesty
  D. Never asking for help

EXPLANATION

Maintain integrity and honesty. Don't try to hide your mistakes from your customer or your boss.

QUESTION 208

The following characteristic constitutes good service in the eyes of most customers:
  A. The technician never asks for help
  B. The technician uses techie language with the customer
  C. The technician visits the customer at least twice
  D. The work is done right the first time

EXPLANATION

The work is done right the first time.

QUESTION 209

The following is true when planning for good customer service:
  A. Almost every support project starts with a phone call or an Internet chat session
  B. Follow your instincts to obtain specific information when answering an initial call
  C. Always recommend an on-site visit
  D. Assume that an on-site visit is always required

EXPLANATION

Almost every support project starts with a phone call or an Internet chat session.

QUESTION 210

The following is true when planning for good customer service:
  A. First troubleshoot, and then review your company's service policies
  B. Keep your company's interests first
  C. Be problem-focused
  D. After reviewing your company's service policies, begin troubleshooting

EXPLANATION

After reviewing your company's service policies, begin troubleshooting.

QUESTION 211

The following is true when planning for good customer service:
A. Always recommend an on-site visit
B. Do not interview the customer about the problem over the phone
C. Ask for help when necessary
D. Never ask for help

EXPLANATION

If you have given the problem your best but still haven't solved it, ask for help.

QUESTION 212

The following is true when making an on-site service call:
A. Plan for at least two on-site visits
B. Arrive with a complete set of equipment that is appropriate to the visit
C. Do not solve the problem over the phone
D. Fill out the paperwork before you start solving the problem

EXPLANATION

Arrive with a complete set of equipment that is appropriate to the visit, which might include a tool kit, flashlight, multimeter, grounding strap and mat, and bootable CDs.

QUESTION 213

The following is true when interacting with the customer:
A. Use first names when addressing your customers
B. Explain to the customer that you need your space to work
C. Fill out the paperwork before you start solving the problem
D. The first thing you should do is listen

EXPLANATION

The first thing you should do is listen; save the paperwork for later.

QUESTION 214

The following is true when interacting with the customer:
A. Interview the customer only once
B. Learn as much as you can about the problem from the customer
C. Always check for user errors first
D. You can make assumptions about the problem

EXPLANATION

Ask the user questions to learn as much as you can about the problem.

2

QUESTION 215

The following is true when making an on-site service call:
  A. Always check for user errors first
  B. Ignore data that has not been backed up
  C. Ask the user about data that is not backed up
  D. Fill out the paperwork before you start troubleshooting

EXPLANATION

Before you begin work, be sure to ask the very important question, "Does the system hold important data that is not backed up?"

QUESTION 216

The following is true when working at a user's desk:
  A. Don't take over the mouse or keyboard from the user without permission
  B. It is acceptable to use the phone without permission
  C. You only need to ask permission to use the phone once
  D. It is acceptable to make software changes without asking for permission

EXPLANATION

If the user is sitting in front of the PC, don't assume you can take over the keyboard or mouse without permission.

QUESTION 217

The following is true when working at the user's desk:
  A. Your needs come before the user's needs
  B. Accept personal inconvenience to accommodate the user's urgent business needs
  C. Help the customer to realize that solving the problem comes first
  D. Use the phone without asking permission first

EXPLANATION

Accept personal inconvenience to accommodate the user's urgent business needs.

QUESTION 218

The following is a good communication skill:
  A. Don't talk down to the user
  B. Patronize the user
  C. Treat your customer as a peer; use techie language as much as possible
  D. Start troubleshooting while the customer explains the problem to you

EXPLANATION

Don't talk down to or patronize the user. Don't make the user feel he or she is inferior.

QUESTION 219

The following is a good communication skill:
- A. Ask your customer permission to make all the important decisions before you start troubleshooting
- B. Be problem-focused
- C. Do not make decisions for your customers
- D. Do not ask for help even if you need it

EXPLANATION

Provide users with alternatives where appropriate before making decisions for them.

QUESTION 220

The following is a good communication skill:
- A. Do not seem eager to solve the problem
- B. Use techie language as much as possible
- C. Be problem-focused
- D. Don't be judgmental or insulting

EXPLANATION

Don't disparage the user's choice of computer hardware or software. Don't be judgmental or insulting.

QUESTION 221

The following is true when the customer is involved with solving the problem:
- A. Explain the problem to the customer and what you must do to fix it
- B. Do not give details about your work to the customer
- C. Never ask the customer for help
- D. It is acceptable to use the phone without asking permission first

EXPLANATION

Explain the problem and what you must do to fix it, giving as many details as the customer wants.

QUESTION 222

Do the following after you have solved a problem:
- A. Close the call as soon as you have solved the problem
- B. Do not keep the customer on the line after you have solved the problem
- C. Do not review the service call with the customer
- D. Allow the customer enough time to be fully satisfied that all is working

EXPLANATION

Allow the customer enough time to be fully satisfied that all is working before you close the call.

QUESTION 223

Do the following after you have solved a problem:

   A. Do not review the service call with the customer
   B. Ask the customer to fill out a report about the work done
   C. Make sure you have not caused a problem with the boot
   D. Close the call as soon as you have solved the problem

EXPLANATION

If you changed anything on the PC after you booted it, reboot one more time to make sure you have not caused a problem with the boot.

QUESTION 224

Do not forget to do the following at the beginning of a service call:

   A. Tell the customer your rates
   B. Identify yourself and your organization
   C. Fill out the paperwork
   D. Recommend an on-site visit

EXPLANATION

Identify yourself and your organization. (Follow the guidelines of your employer on what to say.)

QUESTION 225

Do not forget to do the following at the beginning of a service call:

   A. Fill out the paperwork
   B. Start troubleshooting the problem with the help of the customer
   C. Tell the customer your hours of service
   D. Open up the conversation for the caller to describe the problem

EXPLANATION

Open up the conversation for the caller to describe the problem.

QUESTION 226

The following is true about help-desk support:
- A. Does not require good communication skills
- B. Requires lots of patience
- C. Calls should not last more than 5 minutes
- D. Calls should not last more than 10 minutes

EXPLANATION

Help-desk support requires excellent communication skills, good phone manners, and lots of patience.

QUESTION 227

The following is true when offering phone support:
- A. Earn your customer's sympathy by complaining about your colleagues
- B. If your call is accidentally disconnected, wait for the customer to call back
- C. If your call is accidentally disconnected, call back immediately
- D. It is acceptable to complain about your job with the customer sometimes

EXPLANATION

If your call is accidentally disconnected, call back immediately.

QUESTION 228

The following is true when offering phone support:
- A. Do not eat or drink while on the phone
- B. Complain about your job with the customer
- C. Small talk is not acceptable
- D. If your call is accidentally disconnected, wait for the customer to call back

EXPLANATION

Don't eat or drink while on the phone.

QUESTION 229

The following is true when offering phone support:
- A. Help the customer to describe the problem
- B. A little small talk is acceptable
- C. Close the call as soon as the problem has been solved
- D. It is acceptable to eat or drink while on the phone

EXPLANATION

A little small talk is okay and is sometimes beneficial in easing a tense situation, but keep it upbeat and positive.

QUESTION 230

The following is true when offering phone support
  A. Let the user make sure all is working before you close the phone call
  B. Close the call as soon as the problem has been solved
  C. Small talk is never acceptable
  D. It is acceptable to complain about your job with the customer

EXPLANATION

As with on-site service calls, let the user make sure all is working before you close the phone call.

QUESTION 231

What is the most difficult situation to handle when a customer is not knowledgeable about how to use a computer?
  A. On-site call
  B. E-mail support
  C. Help-desk call
  D. External PC support

EXPLANATION

A help-desk call is the most difficult situation to handle when a customer is not knowledgeable about how to use a computer.

QUESTION 232

The following is true when offering phone support to a customer who is not knowledgeable:
  A. Make the customer feel confident by using techie language
  B. Do not let the customer ask questions
  C. Patronize the customer
  D. Don't use computer jargon while talking

EXPLANATION

Don't use computer jargon while talking. For example, instead of saying, "Open Windows Explorer," say, "Using your mouse, right-click the Start button and select Explore from the menu."

QUESTION 233

The following is true when offering phone support to a customer who is not knowledgeable:
   A. Follow along at your own PC
   B. Ask the user to describe the problem without touching the PC
   C. Use computer jargon while talking
   D. Ask the customer to pass you to a more knowledge user

EXPLANATION

Follow along at your own PC. It's easier to direct the customer, keystroke by keystroke, if you are doing the same things.

QUESTION 234

The following is true when offering phone support to a customer who is overly confident:
   A. Do not ask question about simple things
   B. Assume that you do not need to check for user errors
   C. Do not slow the conversation down
   D. Show respect for the customer's knowledge

EXPLANATION

Show respect for the customer's knowledge. For example, you can ask the customer's advice.

QUESTION 235

The following is true when offering phone support to a customer who is overly confident:
   A. Immediately present your credentials to the customer
   B. Do not use computer jargon while talking with the customer
   C. Slow the conversation down
   D. Ignore the customer's knowledge

EXPLANATION

Slow the conversation down. You can say, "Please slow down. You're moving too fast for me to follow. Help me understand."

2

QUESTION 236

The following is true when offering phone support to a customer who is overly confident:
- A. Do not check for simple things
- B. Do not back off from using problem-solving skills
- C. Do not check for user errors
- D. Back off from using problem-solving skills

EXPLANATION

Don't back off from using problem-solving skills. You must still have the customer check the simple things, but direct the conversation with tact.

QUESTION 237

The following is a suggestion on how to handle complaints and customer anger:
- A. Be a passive listener
- B. Earn the customer's sympathy by complaining about your colleagues
- C. Make others look worse than yourself
- D. Be an active listener

EXPLANATION

Be an active listener, and let customers know they are not being ignored.

QUESTION 238

The following is a suggestion on how to handle complaints and customer anger:
- A. Earn the customer's sympathy by complaining about your company
- B. Don't be defensive
- C. Be a passive listener
- D. Kindly ask the customer to call back when he or she is feeling more calm

EXPLANATION

Don't be defensive. It's better to leave the customer with the impression that you and your company are listening and willing to admit mistakes.

QUESTION 239

The following term describes the right to use software:
- A. Copyright
- B. Installation copy
- C. License
- D. Intellectual property

EXPLANATION

When someone purchases software from a software vendor, that person has only pur-chased a license for the software, which is the right to use it.

QUESTION 240

The following term describes the right to copy the work and belongs to the creator of the work:

A. Copyright
B. License
C. Site license
D. Campus agreement

EXPLANATION

The right to copy the work, called a copyright, belongs to the creator of the work or others to whom the creator transfers this right.

ANSWER GRID FOR COMPTIA A+ 220-602

Question	Answer	Objective	Question	Answer	Objective
1	B	3.1	35	C	1.3
2	A	3.1	36	A	1.3
3	B	3.1	37	B	1.3
4	A	3.1	38	D	1.3
5	A	3.1	39	A	7.1
6	D	3.1	40	D	7.1
7	D	3.1	41	C	7.1
8	A	3.1	42	B	7.1
9	C	3.1	43	D	1.2
10	B	3.1	44	C	1.2
11	C	3.1	45	D	1.2
12	B	3.1	46	C	1.2
13	A	3.1	47	D	1.2
14	D	3.1	48	A	1.2
15	A	3.3	49	D	1.2
16	C	3.3	50	B	1.2
17	D	3.3	51	D	1.2
18	B	3.3	52	C	1.3
19	C	3.3	53	A	1.3
20	B	3.3	54	B	1.3
21	D	1.2	55	A	1.3
22	A	1.2	56	B	1.3
23	D	1.2	57	D	1.3
24	B	7.1	58	C	1.3
25	A	7.1	59	A	1.3
26	C	7.1	60	B	1.3
27	B	7.1	61	C	1.2
28	D	7.1	62	D	1.1–1.2
29	C	7.1	63	B	1.1–1.2
30	A	7.1	64	C	1.1–1.2
31	D	7.1	65	A	1.1–1.3
32	A	7.1	66	D	1.1
33	C	4.4	67	B	1.1
34	B	4.4	68	D	1.1

2

Question	Answer	Objective	Question	Answer	Objective
69	A	1.3	105	D	3.1
70	B	1.3	106	B	3.1
71	C	1.3	107	A	3.1
72	B	1.3	108	C	3.1
73	D	1.3	109	B	3.1
74	A	1.3	110	C	3.1
75	B	1.1	111	A	3.1
76	A	1.1	112	D	3.1
77	C	6.2	113	A	3.2
78	A	6.2	114	C	3.2
79	A	2.1	115	D	3.2
80	D	2.1	116	B	3.1
81	B	2.1	117	C	3.1
82	C	2.1	118	B	3.2–3.3
83	A	2.1	119	A	3.1, 3.3
84	C	2.1	120	D	3.1, 3.4
85	B	2.1	121	A	3.3–3.4
86	D	2.1	122	C	3.1, 3.4
87	C	2.2	123	D	3.1, 3.4
88	D	2.2	124	B	3.3, 3.4
89	B	2.2	125	C	3.1
90	A	2.2	126	B	3.1–3.3
91	D	5.1	127	A	3.1–3.3
92	A	5.1	128	D	3.2
93	B	5.1	129	B	6.1–6.2
94	C	5.1	130	D	6.1–6.2
95	A	2.3	131	A	5.2–5.3
96	C	2.3	132	C	5.2–5.3
97	D	2.3	133	D	6.1–6.2
98	B	2.3	134	C	6.1–6.2
99	C	1.1	135	B	5.2–5.3
100	B	1.1	136	A	5.2–5.3
101	D	5.2	137	B	5.2–5.3
102	A	5.2	138	D	5.2–5.3
103	C	5.2	139	A	6.1–6.2
104	B	5.2	140	C	6.1–6.2

Question	Answer	Objective	Question	Answer	Objective
141	B	3.1–3.4	177	D	4.1
142	D	3.1–3.4	178	B	4.1
143	C	3.1–3.4	179	B	4.1
144	A	5.2	180	A	4.1
145	D	5.1, 5.3	181	C	4.2
146	A	5.1, 5.3	182	A	4.2
147	C	6.2–6.3	183	D	4.2
148	B	5.1	184	B	4.2
149	A	5.1	185	D	4.2
150	B	5.1	186	B	4.2
151	C	5.1	187	C	4.3–4.4
152	D	5.2–5.3	188	A	4.3–4.4
153	B	6.2–6.3	189	C	4.3–4.4
154	D	6.2–6.3	190	D	4.3–4.4
155	C	6.2–6.3	191	A	4.3–4.4
156	A	6.2–6.3	192	B	4.3–4.4
157	B	6.2–6.3	193	D	4.3–4.4
158	A	5.1	194	B	4.3–4.4
159	C	5.1	195	A	4.3–4.4
160	D	5.3	196	C	4.3–4.4
161	A	5.3	197	A	4.3–4.4
162	D	6.2–6.3	198	D	4.3–4.4
163	C	6.2–6.3	199	C	4.3–4.4
164	B	6.2–6.3	200	B	4.3–4.4
165	D	6.1–6.3	201	D	4.3–4.4
166	B	6.1–6.3	202	B	4.3–4.4
167	C	6.1–6.3	203	C	4.3–4.4
168	A	2.2	204	A	4.3–4.4
169	B	2.2	205	B	8.1–8.2
170	A	2.2	206	A	8.1–8.2
171	C	2.2	207	C	8.1–8.2
172	D	2.2	208	D	8.1–8.2
173	A	2.2	209	A	8.1–8.2
174	D	4.1	210	D	8.1–8.2
175	B	4.1	211	C	8.1–8.2
176	C	4.1	212	B	8.1–8.2

Question	Answer	Objective	Question	Answer	Objective
213	D	8.1–8.2	227	C	8.1–8.2
214	B	8.1–8.2	228	A	8.1–8.2
215	C	8.1–8.2	229	B	8.1–8.2
216	A	8.1–8.2	230	A	8.1–8.2
217	B	8.1–8.2	231	C	8.1–8.2
218	A	8.1–8.2	232	D	8.1–8.2
219	C	8.1–8.2	233	A	8.1–8.2
220	D	8.1–8.2	234	D	8.1–8.2
221	A	8.1–8.2	235	C	8.1–8.2
222	D	8.1–8.2	236	B	8.1–8.2
223	C	8.1–8.2	237	D	8.1–8.2
224	B	8.1–8.2	238	B	8.1–8.2
225	D	8.1–8.2	239	C	8.1–8.2
226	B	8.1–8.2	240	A	8.1–8.2

CompTIA A+ 220-603

QUESTION 1

The following is a hidden Windows 2000/XP text file that contains information about installed OSs on the loader program hard drive:

A. Boot.ini

B. Config.sys

C. Autoexec.bat

D. Msconfig.ini

EXPLANATION

Boot.ini is a hidden text file that contains information about installed OSs on the loader program hard drive.

QUESTION 2

In Windows 2000/XP, the following program is responsible for loading an OS other than Windows:

A. Boot.ini

B. Msloader.exe

C. Loader.sys

D. Bootsect.dos

EXPLANATION

Bootsect.dos is responsible for loading the other OS.

QUESTION 3

In Windows 2000/XP, the following file is required only if a SCSI boot device is used:

A. Ntdetect.com

B. Ntbootdd.sys

C. Ntdll.dll

D. Hal.dll

EXPLANATION

Ntbootdd.sys is required only if a SCSI boot device is used.

QUESTION 4

In Windows 2000/XP, the following file is the virtual memory swap file:

A. Gdi32.dll
B. Ntdll.dll
C. Pagefile.sys
D. Advapi32.dll

EXPLANATION

Pagefile.sys is the virtual memory swap file.

QUESTION 5

In what directory are most Windows system files stored?

A. C:\Windows\System32\
B. C:\System\Windows
C. C:\System\32\Windows
D. C:\Windows 32\System

EXPLANATION

Most Windows system files are stored in the C:\Windows\System32\ folder.

QUESTION 6

In Windows 2000/XP, the following directory contains the registry hives:

A. C:\Program Files
B. C:\Windows\System32\drivers
C. C:\Windows\System32\config
D. C:\Documents and Settings

EXPLANATION

C:\Windows\System32\config contains the registry hives.

QUESTION 7

The Boot.ini file can contain the following switch to configure Data Execute Prevention (DEP):

A. /NoRun
B. /NoExecute
C. /DisableExecute
D. /StopRun

EXPLANATION

The Boot.ini file can contain the /NoExecute switch to configure Data Execute Prevention (DEP).

QUESTION 8

The following Windows 2000/XP feature stops a program if it oversteps its boundaries in memory:

A. Memory Overrun Protection (MOP)

B. System Overstep Boundaries (SOB)

C. Monitor Memory Use (MMU)

D. Data Execute Prevention (DEP)

EXPLANATION

Data Execute Prevention (DEP) stops a program if it oversteps its boundaries in memory.

QUESTION 9

The following Windows 2000/XP tool is used to stop or start a service that runs in the background:

A. Runas.exe

B. Msconfig.exe

C. Sc.exe

D. Sfc.exe

EXPLANATION

SC (Sc.exe) is used to stop or start a service that runs in the background.

QUESTION 10

The following Windows 2000/XP tool is used to list and stop currently running processes:

A. Task Lister

B. Windows File Protection

C. Windows Update

D. Task Manager

EXPLANATION

Task Manager (Taskman.exe) is used to list and stop currently running processes.

QUESTION 11

The following menu can be used to diagnose and fix problems when booting Windows 2000/XP:

A. Advanced Options

B. Boot

C. Startup

D. Init

EXPLANATION

The Windows 2000/XP Advanced Options menu can be used to diagnose and fix problems when booting Windows 2000/XP.

QUESTION 12

When you load Windows 2000/XP in Safe Mode, all files used for the load are recorded in the following file:

A. Ntldr.txt

B. Ntbtlog.txt

C. Boot.log.txt

D. Bootlog.txt

EXPLANATION

When you load Windows 2000/XP in Safe Mode, all files used for the load are recorded in the Ntbtlog.txt file.

QUESTION 13

When you boot with this option, Windows 2000/XP loads normally, and you access the regular desktop.

A. Safe Mode

B. Safe Mode with Networking

C. Safe Mode with Command Prompt

D. Enable Boot Logging

EXPLANATION

When you boot with the Enable Boot Logging option, Windows 2000/XP loads normally, and you access the regular desktop.

QUESTION 14

Where does Windows 2000/XP keep the Last Known Good configuration?

A. Ntbtlog.txt

B. Registry

C. Msconfig.sys

D. Config.sys

EXPLANATION

Windows 2000/XP keeps the Last Known Good configuration in the registry.

QUESTION 15

By default, Windows 2000/XP automatically restarts immediately after it encounters a system failure, which is also called:

A. Debug screen

B. Controller window

C. Blue screen of death

D. Last known good screen

EXPLANATION

By default, Windows 2000/XP automatically restarts immediately after it encounters a system failure, which is also called a stop error or a blue screen of death (BSOD).

QUESTION 16

You can use the following troubleshooting tool when Windows 2000/XP does not start properly or hangs during the load:

A. Recovery Console

B. Dr. Pc Console

C. Debug Console

D. BSOD Console

EXPLANATION

Use the Recovery Console when Windows 2000/XP does not start properly or hangs during the load.

QUESTION 17

The following Recovery Console command carries out commands stored in a batch file:

A. Script

B. Batch

C. Copy

D. Cls

EXPLANATION

Batch carries out commands stored in a batch file.

QUESTION 18

The following Recovery Console command creates and deletes partitions on the hard drive:

  A. Diskpart
  B. Expand
  C. Fixboot
  D. Fixmbr

EXPLANATION

Diskpart creates and deletes partitions on the hard drive.

QUESTION 19

The Following Recovery Console command rewrites the Master Boot Record boot program:

  A. Fixboot
  B. Format
  C. Fixmbr
  D. Diskpart

EXPLANATION

Fixmbr rewrites the Master Boot Record boot program.

QUESTION 20

The following Recovery Console command displays or sets Recovery Console environmental variables:

  A. Map
  B. Listsvc
  C. Systemroot
  D. Set

EXPLANATION

Set displays or sets Recovery Console environmental variables.

QUESTION 21

The following Recovery Console command makes the Windows folder the current folder:

A. Systemroot
B. Listsrv
C. Ren
D. Fdisk

EXPLANATION

Systemroot makes the Windows folder the current folder.

QUESTION 22

The following Recovery Console command lists all services currently installed:

A. Ren
B. Cls
C. Fixboot
D. Listsvc

EXPLANATION

Enter the command Listsvc to see a list of all services currently installed, which includes device drivers.

QUESTION 23

The following Recovery Console command displays the current drive letters:

A. Ren
B. Dir
C. Map
D. Set

EXPLANATION

Map displays the current drive letters.

QUESTION 24

The following Recovery Console command lets you view and edit the Boot.ini file:

A. Map
B. Bootcfg
C. Fixboot
D. Set

EXPLANATION

Bootcfg lets you view and edit the Boot.ini file.

QUESTION 25

The program in the MBR displays this message when it cannot find the active partition on the hard drive or the boot sector on that partition:

A. Inaccessible boot device
B. Hard drive not found
C. Fixed disk error
D. No boot device available

EXPLANATION

The program in the MBR displays the "Inaccessible boot device" message when it cannot find the active partition on the hard drive or the boot sector on that partition.

QUESTION 26

The following type of error is likely to be a corrupted MBR, partition table, boot sector, or Ntldr file:

A. Invalid boot disk
B. Black screen with no error messages
C. Invalid partition table
D. Fixed disk error

EXPLANATION

A black screen with no error messages is likely to be a corrupted MBR, partition table, boot sector, or Ntldr file.

QUESTION 27

Why would you get the "Stop 0x00000024" error message?

A. A disk is in the floppy drive
B. RAM is defective
C. NTFS file system is corrupted
D. Bad sector on the hard drive

EXPLANATION

"Stop 0x00000024" means the NTFS file system is corrupted.

QUESTION 28

The following type of error is so drastic that it causes Windows to hang or lock up:

A. USB error
B. LED error
C. Blue error
D. Stop error

EXPLANATION

One type of error message is a stop error, which is an error so drastic that it causes Windows to hang or lock up.

QUESTION 29

To keep programs kept in startup folders from executing as you start Windows, hold down the following key just after you enter your account name and password on the Windows logon screen:

   A. Esc

   B. Shift

   C. Alt

   D. Ctrl

EXPLANATION

To keep programs kept in startup folders from executing as you start Windows, hold down the Shift key just after you enter your account name and password on the Windows logon screen.

QUESTION 30

In Windows 2000/XP, tasks that are scheduled to launch at startup are placed in this folder:

   A. C:\Startup

   B. C:\System\Tasks

   C. C:\System32\Tasks

   D. C:\Windows\Tasks

EXPLANATION

Tasks that are scheduled to launch at startup are placed in this folder: C:\Windows\Tasks.

QUESTION 31

When an administrator uses Group Policy to cause a script to run, Group Policy places that script in one of the folders in the following list:

   A. C:\Windows\Tasks

   B. C:\Windows\System32\Policy

   C. C:\Windows\System32\GroupPolicy\User\Scripts\Logon

   D. C:\Program Files\Policy\Groups

EXPLANATION

Group Policy places scripts in one of the following folders:

C:\Windows\System32\GroupPolicy\Machine\Scripts\Startup

C:\Windows\System32\GroupPolicy\Machine\Scripts\Shutdown

C:\Windows\System32\GroupPolicy\User\Scripts\Logon

C:\Windows\System32\GroupPolicy\User\Scripts\Logoff

QUESTION 32

In which folder does Windows 2000/XP store all installed fonts?
  A. C:\Windows\Fonts
  B. C:\System\Fonts
  C. C:\System32\Fonts
  D. C:\Fonts

EXPLANATION

Windows 2000/XP stores all installed fonts in the C:\Windows\Fonts folder.

QUESTION 33

The following type of network consists of personal devices at close range:
  A. LAN
  B. WiMax
  C. PAN
  D. MAN

EXPLANATION

A PAN (personal area network) consists of personal devices at close range, such as a cell phone, PDA, and notebook computer in communication.

QUESTION 34

The following type of network covers a small local area such as a home, office, or other building or small group of buildings:
  A. PAN
  B. MAN
  C. WiMAX
  D. LAN

EXPLANATION

A LAN (local area network) covers a small local area such as a home, office, or other building or small group of buildings.

QUESTION 35

The following type of network covers a large campus or city:

A. MAN
B. WAN
C. WiMAX
D. Wi-Fi

EXPLANATION

A MAN (metropolitan area network) covers a large campus or city.

QUESTION 36

The following type of network covers a large geographical area and is made up of many smaller networks:

A. PAN
B. WAN
C. LAN
D. MAN

EXPLANATION

A WAN (wide area network) covers a large geographical area and is made up of many smaller networks.

QUESTION 37

The amount of data that can travel over a given communication system in a given amount of time is called:

A. Network size
B. Data size
C. Channel width
D. Line speed

EXPLANATION

This measure of data capacity is called bandwidth (or data throughput or line speed).

QUESTION 38

The following term refers to a networking technology that carries more than one type of signal, such as DSL and telephone:

A. Bandwidth
B. Broadband
C. T1 band
D. Line carrier

EXPLANATION

Broadband refers to a networking technology that carries more than one type of signal, such as DSL and telephone.

QUESTION 39

What is the IEEE standard that applies to networking?

A. IEEE 802
B. IEEE 810
C. IEEE 812
D. IEEE 815

EXPLANATION

The IEEE 802 standard applies to networking.

QUESTION 40

The following term refers to a device on the network:

A. NIC
B. Port
C. Node
D. Socket

EXPLANATION

A node, or host, is one device on the network.

QUESTION 41

The following term is used to describe a network adapter 48-bit number that identifies the adapter on the network:

A. IP address
B. MAC address
C. Logical address
D. Router address

EXPLANATION

The number is often written in hex and is called the MAC (Media Access Control) address, hardware address, physical address, adapter address, or Ethernet address.

QUESTION 42

The following term refers to the rules used for communication on a network:

A. Host
B. Adapter policy
C. Network protocol
D. Socket rules

EXPLANATION

Communication on a network follows rules of communication called network protocols.

QUESTION 43

Apple Computer uses the following term to refer to 802.11b:

A. AirNet
B. WiPort
C. WiNet
D. AirPort

EXPLANATION

Apple Computer calls 802.11b AirPort, and it calls 802.11g AirPort Extreme.

QUESTION 44

The following standard defines how wireless network traffic can better be distributed over multiple access points:

A. 802.11k
B. 802.11n
C. 802.11s
D. 802.11x

EXPLANATION

The 802.11k standard defines how wireless network traffic can better be distributed over multiple access points covering a wide area so that the access point with the strongest signal is not overloaded.

QUESTION 45

WiMAX is defined under the following IEEE standards:

A. 802.11a and 802.11b
B. 802.11b and 802.11g
C. 802.16d and 802.16e
D. 802.20a and 802.20i

EXPLANATION

A newer IEEE wireless standard is WiMAX, which is defined under IEEE 802.16d and 802.16e.

QUESTION 46

Which command can you use in Windows XP to display your MAC address?
  A. Getmac
  B. Ipaddress
  C. Getaddress
  D. Macaddress

EXPLANATION

If you're running Windows XP Professional, you can also display your MAC address using the Getmac command.

QUESTION 47

The following is one of the most powerful and versatile methods of communicating over a network:
  A. Client for Microsoft Networks
  B. NetBIOS
  C. IPX/SPX
  D. Network drive map

EXPLANATION

A network drive map is one of the most powerful and versatile methods of communicating over a network.

QUESTION 48

The following term describes a computer that does nothing but provide hard drive storage on a network for other computers:
  A. Mail server
  B. File server
  C. Domain controller
  D. DNS server

EXPLANATION

A computer that does nothing but provide hard drive storage on a network for other computers is called a file server or a network attached storage (NAS) device.

QUESTION 49

The following is one of the three main methods of encryption for 802.11 wireless networks:

A. WEP
B. RSA
C. Blowfish
D. Bluefish

EXPLANATION

The three main methods of encryption for 802.11 wireless networks are WEP (Wired Equivalent Privacy), WPA (WiFi Protected Access), and WPA2.

QUESTION 50

The following is one way to protect a wireless network:

A. Broadcast the SSID
B. Change the firmware default settings
C. Use the firmware default settings
D. Set the SSID as the brand name of the device

EXPLANATION

Change the firmware default settings to protect a wireless network. The default settings are easy to guess.

QUESTION 51

The following Windows 2000/XP tool allows you to manually control network routing tables:

A. Ipconfig
B. ARP
C. Tracert
D. Route

EXPLANATION

Route allows you to manually control network routing tables.

QUESTION 52

The following program is an example of firewall software:

A. Mozilla
B. Firefox
C. ZoneAlarm
D. AVTrust

3

EXPLANATION

ZoneAlarm by Zone Labs is an example of firewall software.

QUESTION 53

Of these four protocols—PPTP, L2TP, SSL, and IPSec—which is the weakest?
  A. L2TP
  B. PPTP
  C. SSL
  D. IPSec

EXPLANATION

Of the four, PPTP is the weakest protocol and should not be used if one of the other three is available.

QUESTION 54

What is the strongest tunneling protocol?
  A. PPTP
  B. SSL
  C. L2TP over IPSec
  D. SSL over PPTP

EXPLANATION

The strongest protocol is a combination of L2TP and IPSec, which is called L2TP over IPSec.

QUESTION 55

The following Windows XP Professional tool gives a user access to his or her Windows XP desktop from anywhere on the Internet:
  A. Remote Desktop
  B. Network Console
  C. Remote Console
  D. Network Desktop

EXPLANATION

Windows XP Professional Remote Desktop gives a user access to his or her Windows XP desktop from anywhere on the Internet.

QUESTION 56

The following term refers to methods for proving that an individual is who he says he is:

A. Authorization
B. Integrity
C. Confidentiality
D. Authentication

EXPLANATION

Authentication proves that an individual is who he says he is.

QUESTION 57

The following type of passwords are assigned in CMOS setup to prevent unauthorized access to the computer and/or to the CMOS setup utility:

A. Screensaver password
B. Hibernation password
C. Power-on password
D. Windows password

EXPLANATION

Power-on passwords are assigned in CMOS setup to prevent unauthorized access to the computer and/or to the CMOS setup utility.

QUESTION 58

The following is true about passwords and passphrases:

A. A passphrase is easier to remember than a password
B. A password is easier to remember than a passphrase
C. A password is generally made of several words
D. A strong password has up to eight characters

EXPLANATION

If your system allows it, a passphrase rather than a password is easier to remember and harder to guess.

QUESTION 59

Using Windows, controlling access to a computer or the resources on that computer is accomplished with the following:

A. Web browser and SSL
B. HTTPS
C. EAP and digital certificates
D. User accounts and passwords

EXPLANATION

Using Windows, controlling access to a computer or the resources on that computer is accomplished with user accounts and passwords.

QUESTION 60

The following is true about firewalls:
  A. Software firewalls are better than hardware firewalls
  B. Software firewalls are better than no firewall at all
  C. Software firewalls are foolproof
  D. Software firewalls are not supported by Windows XP

EXPLANATION

Software firewalls are better than no firewall at all.

QUESTION 61

The following is one way to protect files and folders in Windows 2000/XP:
  A. Encrypted File System
  B. AEP
  C. NTFS
  D. LFS

EXPLANATION

One way that you can protect files and folders is to use the Windows 2000/XP Encrypted File System (EFS).

QUESTION 62

The following puts data into code that must be translated before it can be accessed and can be applied to either a folder or a file:
  A. Authorization
  B. Encryption
  C. Authentication
  D. Integrity

EXPLANATION

Encryption puts data into code that must be translated before it can be accessed and can be applied to either a folder or a file.

QUESTION 63

The following statement is true:
- A. You can share encrypted folders
- B. You cannot share encrypted files
- C. You must share encrypted folders
- D. You cannot share encrypted folders

EXPLANATION

You cannot share encrypted folders, but you can share encrypted files.

QUESTION 64

The following command can be used from a Windows 2000/XP command prompt to encrypt a large number of files or folders:
- A. Protect
- B. Encrypt
- C. Scramble
- D. Cipher

EXPLANATION

If you are encrypting a large number of files or folders from a command prompt or using a batch file, you can use the Cipher command.

QUESTION 65

The following term describes the practice of tricking people into giving out private information or allowing unsafe programs into the network or computer:
- A. Spam
- B. Social engineering
- C. Trojans
- D. Malware

EXPLANATION

Social engineering is the practice of tricking people into giving out private information or allowing unsafe programs into the network or computer.

QUESTION 66

The following is a type of identity theft where the sender of an e-mail message scams you into responding with personal data about yourself:
- A. Adware
- B. Spyware
- C. Phishing
- D. Spam

3

EXPLANATION

Phishing is a type of identity theft where the sender of an e-mail message scams you into responding with personal data about yourself.

QUESTION 67

You can track logging on to a standalone computer or a computer in a workgroup by using the following Windows 2000/XP tool:

A. Event Viewer
B. Management Console
C. Command Console
D. Log Management

EXPLANATION

You can track logging on to a standalone computer or a computer in a workgroup by using Event Viewer.

QUESTION 68

You can use the following Windows 2000/XP tool to monitor and log network activity:

A. Event Viewer
B. Network Connections
C. Network Events
D. Windows Firewall

EXPLANATION

You can use Windows Firewall to monitor and log network activity.

QUESTION 69

Most manufacturers or retailers of notebooks offer warranty for at least:

A. One year
B. Two years
C. Three years
D. Four years

EXPLANATION

Most manufacturers or retailers of notebooks offer at least a one-year warranty.

QUESTION 70

The following can void your notebook warranty:

A. Taking it to an authorized service center
B. Buying an extended warranty
C. Opening the case
D. Refusing to buy an extended warranty

EXPLANATION

Warranties can be voided by opening the case, removing part labels, installing other-vendor parts, upgrading the OS, or disassembling the system unless directly instructed to do so by the service center help desk personnel.

QUESTION 71

The following is true about notebooks:

A. Notebooks come without an OS installed
B. You cannot replace a notebook OS
C. The only OS that can be installed on a notebook is OEM
D. Notebooks come with an OS preinstalled at the factory

EXPLANATION

Notebook computers are sold with an operating system preinstalled at the factory.

QUESTION 72

The following is a Windows 9x/Me system folder used to synchronize files between two computers:

A. Event Viewer
B. Briefcase
C. Channel Aggregation
D. Folder Redirection

EXPLANATION

Windows 9x/Me Briefcase is a system folder used to synchronize files between two computers.

QUESTION 73

The following Windows 2000/XP feature lets you point to an alternate location on a network for a folder.

A. Briefcase
B. Offline Files and Folder
C. Folder redirection
D. Hardware profiles

EXPLANATION

Folder redirection lets you point to an alternate location on a network for a folder.

QUESTION 74

The following Windows 2000/XP feature lets you specify which devices are to be loaded on startup for a particular user or set of circumstances:

   A. Folder redirection

   B. Hardware profiles

   C. Briefcase

   D. Offline Files and Folders

EXPLANATION

Hardware profiles let you specify which devices are to be loaded on startup for a particular user or set of circumstances.

QUESTION 75

The following is true about notebooks:

   A. Notebooks tend to last longer than desktop PCs

   B. Desktop PCs are more susceptible to viruses than notebook systems

   C. Desktop PCs are subjected to more wear and tear

   D. Notebooks tend to last a shorter time than desktop PCs

EXPLANATION

Notebook computers tend not to last as long as desktop computers because they are portable and, therefore, subjected to more wear and tear.

QUESTION 76

The following is a good notebook care guideline:

   A. Protect a notebook against ESD

   B. You can connect a modem in a notebook to a PBX

   C. It is good to power a notebook up and down constantly

   D. You can leave a notebook in a dusty or smoke-filled area

EXPLANATION

Protect a notebook against ESD.

QUESTION 77

How wide is a desktop hard drive?

A. 1 inch
B. 1.5 inches
C. 2.5 inches
D. 3.5 inches

EXPLANATION

A desktop hard drive is 3.5 inches wide.

QUESTION 78

Most IDE notebook hard drives sold today use the following type of connector:

A. Universal 32-pin
B. SATA 72-pin
C. Universal 40-pin
D. SATA 144-pin

EXPLANATION

Most notebook hard drives sold today use a universal 40-pin connector for an IDE notebook.

QUESTION 79

What is the first step to troubleshoot a notebook problem?

A. Interview the user
B. Remove the battery pack
C. Unplug the power cord
D. Remove any CD or DVD

EXPLANATION

When troubleshooting a notebook problem, begin by interviewing the user.

QUESTION 80

When troubleshooting a notebook AC adapter, the following is true:

A. The voltage range should be plus or minus 2 percent of the accepted voltage
B. The voltage range should be plus or minus 5 percent of the accepted voltage
C. The voltage range should be plus or minus 10 percent of the accepted voltage
D. The voltage range should be plus or minus 20 percent of the accepted voltage

EXPLANATION

The voltage range should be plus or minus 5 percent of the accepted voltage.

QUESTION 81

Notebook manufacturers sometimes call the battery that powers CMOS RAM the following:

A. RAM battery
B. Dynamic battery
C. Backup battery
D. Notebook battery

EXPLANATION

Notebook manufacturers sometimes call this battery the backup battery or reserve battery.

QUESTION 82

For Windows 2000/XP, you can boot to the Advanced Options menu by pressing the following key during the boot:

A. F5
B. F8
C. F10
D. F12

EXPLANATION

For Windows 2000/XP, try booting to the Advanced Options menu by pressing F8 during the boot.

QUESTION 83

The following is true when troubleshooting power problems on a notebook:

A. If backup batteries need replacing often, replace the motherboard
B. If backup batteries need replacing often, replace the LCD
C. If backup batteries need replacing often, replace the DC controller
D. If backup batteries need replacing often, replace the main battery

EXPLANATION

If backup batteries need replacing often, replace the motherboard.

QUESTION 84

If your notebook gets wet, allow it and the components to dry for:

A. 2 hours
B. At most 5 hours
C. At most 24 hours
D. At least 24 hours

EXPLANATION

If the notebook gets wet, allow the notebook and all components to dry for at least 24 hours at room temperature.

QUESTION 85

The following kit can be used to install a notebook hard drive in a desktop system:
A. PC Cables
B. Notebook IDE adapter
C. USB-to-PCI adapter
D. IDE-to-SATA adapter

EXPLANATION

A notebook IDE adapter kit can be used to install a notebook hard drive in a desktop system.

QUESTION 86

The following is true when troubleshooting a notebook:
A. Intermittent problems are always caused by software
B. Intermittent problems are always caused by hardware
C. Intermittent problems are never caused by software
D. Intermittent problems might be caused by hardware

EXPLANATION

Intermittent problems might or might not have to do with hardware.

QUESTION 87

The following term describes the time that it takes for the first page to print:
A. Warm-up time
B. DPI time
C. GDI time
D. PCL time

EXPLANATION

The time that it takes for the first page to print is called the warm-up time.

QUESTION 88

The following is a type of electrophotographic printer:
A. Thermal printer
B. Dot matrix printer
C. Laser printer
D. Impact printer

EXPLANATION

A laser printer is a type of electrophotographic printer that can range from a small, personal desktop model to a large, network printer capable of handling and printing large volumes continuously.

QUESTION 89

In what step of the printing process for a laser printer does a laser beam discharge a lower charge only to places where toner should go?

A. Cleaning
B. Fusing
C. Developing
D. Writing

EXPLANATION

In the writing step, a laser beam discharges a lower charge only to places where toner should go.

QUESTION 90

In what step of the printing process for a laser printer is toner placed on the drum where the charge has been reduced?

A. Conditioning
B. Fusing
C. Developing
D. Writing

EXPLANATION

In the developing process, toner is placed on the drum where the charge has been reduced.

QUESTION 91

The following type of printer uses a type of ink-dispersion printing:

A. Thermal printer
B. Ink-jet printer
C. Dot matrix printer
D. Dye sublimation printer

EXPLANATION

Ink-jet printers use a type of ink-dispersion printing.

QUESTION 92

The following type of printer uses wax-based ink that is heated by heat pins that melt the ink onto paper:

A. Thermal printer
B. Dot matrix printer
C. Laser printer
D. Ink-jet printer

EXPLANATION

Thermal printers use wax-based ink that is heated by heat pins that melt the ink onto paper.

QUESTION 93

The following is a device that allows a computer to convert a picture, drawing, bar code, or other image into digital data that can be input into the computer as a file:

A. Printer
B. Thermal drum
C. Scanner
D. Optic pen

EXPLANATION

A scanner is a device that allows a computer to convert a picture, drawing, bar code, or other image into digital data that can be input into the computer as a file.

QUESTION 94

The following term refers to a printer accessed by way of a network:

A. Network printer
B. Hot-pluggable printer
C. Default printer
D. Local printer

EXPLANATION

A printer accessed by way of a network is called a network printer.

QUESTION 95

In Windows 2000/XP, you can install a local printer with the following tool:

A. System tray
B. Device console
C. Hardware Properties Wizard
D. Add Printer Wizard

EXPLANATION

In Windows 2000/XP, you can install a local printer with the Add Printer Wizard from the Printer and Faxes window.

QUESTION 96

When installing a network printer, you can enter the printer name using the following format:
    A. \host-name\\printer-name
    B. \\host-name\printer-name
    C. /printer-name/host-name//
    D. \\host-name//printer-name

EXPLANATION

Enter the host computer name and printer name. Begin with two backslashes, and separate the computer name from the printer name with a backslash.

QUESTION 97

The following device can control several printers that are connected to a network:
    A. Print server
    B. Ink server
    C. Direct server
    D. Network printer

EXPLANATION

A dedicated device or computer called a print server can control several printers that are connected to a network.

QUESTION 98

The following language draws and formats the page and then sends the almost-ready-to-print page to the printer in bitmap form:
    A. PCL
    B. GDI
    C. PostScript
    D. PS

EXPLANATION

GDI draws and formats the page and then sends the almost-ready-to-print page to the printer in bitmap form.

QUESTION 99

The following is true when dealing with customers:
- A. It is easier to deal with customers who are technically knowledgeable
- B. Only deal with customers who pay their bills promptly
- C. It is easier to deal with customers who are technically naive
- D. Nothing should affect your commitment to excellence

EXPLANATION

Don't allow circumstances or personalities to affect your commitment to excellence.

QUESTION 100

The following trait distinguishes one competent technician from another in the eyes of the customer:
- A. Keep your company's interests first
- B. Never call for help
- C. Be customer-focused
- D. Be problem-focused

EXPLANATION

When you're working with or talking to a customer, focus on him or her.

QUESTION 101

The following trait distinguishes one competent technician from another in the eyes of the customer:
- A. Never make customers repeat themselves
- B. Act professionally
- C. Behave casually
- D. Be a passive listener

EXPLANATION

Act professionally. Customers want a technician to look and behave professionally.

QUESTION 102

The following characteristic constitutes good service in the eyes of most customers:
- A. Problems are always solved after an on-site visit
- B. The price for the work is always higher than the average
- C. The price for the work is reasonable
- D. The technician planned at least two on-site visits

EXPLANATION

The price for the work is reasonable and competitive.

QUESTION 103

The following is true when planning for good customer service:
- A. Always recommend an on-site visit
- B. Assume that an on-site visit is always necessary
- C. Keep your company's interests first
- D. Don't assume that an on-site visit is always necessary

EXPLANATION

Don't assume that an on-site visit is necessary until you have asked questions to identify the problem and asked the caller to check and try some simple things while on the phone with you.

QUESTION 104

The following is true when planning for good customer service:
- A. Search for answers
- B. Never call for help
- C. Be problem-focused
- D. Tell the user not to touch anything until the technician arrives

EXPLANATION

Search for answers. If the answers to specific questions or problems are not evident, become a researcher.

QUESTION 105

The following is true when planning for good customer service:
- A. Do not keep the user on the line after you have solved the problem
- B. The technician should end the call or chat session
- C. Allow the customer to decide when the service is finished
- D. Fill out the paperwork before you start troubleshooting

EXPLANATION

When you think you've solved the problem, allow the customer to decide when the service is finished to his or her satisfaction.

QUESTION 106

The following is true when making an on-site service call:
- A. Set a realistic time for the appointment
- B. Arrive at least 20 minutes before the actual appointment time
- C. Always use first names when addressing your customers
- D. Instruct the customer that you need your space to work

EXPLANATION

Set a realistic time for the appointment (one that you can expect to keep), and arrive on time.

QUESTION 107

The following is true when interacting with the customer:
- A. Instruct the customer that you need your space to work
- B. Be problem-focused
- C. Be a passive listener; let the customer do the talking
- D. Be as unobtrusive as possible

EXPLANATION

As you work, be as unobtrusive as possible. Don't make a big mess.

QUESTION 108

The following is true when interacting with the customer:
- A. Do not make customers repeat themselves
- B. Ask the customer to listen while you repeat the problem
- C. Do not ask the customer questions that have already been asked
- D. Instruct the customer that you need your space to work

EXPLANATION

Ask the user to listen while you repeat the problem to make sure you understand it correctly.

QUESTION 109

The following is true when interacting with the customer:
- A. Use diplomacy and good manners
- B. Check for user errors first
- C. Assume that the customer caused the problem
- D. It is acceptable to interrupt the customer as long as you ask questions regarding the problem at hand

3

EXPLANATION

Use diplomacy and good manners when you work with a user to solve a problem.

QUESTION 110

The following is true when working at the user's desk:
  A. It is acceptable to take over the mouse or keyboard without asking permission
  B. Ask permission before you use the printer or other equipment
  C. Instruct the customer that you need your space to work
  D. Be as obtrusive as possible

EXPLANATION

Ask permission before you use the printer or other equipment.

QUESTION 111

The following is a good communication technique:
  A. Interrupt the user constantly
  B. Treat the customer as your peer; use techie language as much as possible
  C. Be a passive listener
  D. Be a good listener

EXPLANATION

When you ask the user to describe the problem, be a good listener. Don't interrupt.

QUESTION 112

The following is a good communication skill:
  A. Treat the customer as your peer; use techie language as much as possible
  B. Help the customer to understand that solving the problem is the first priority
  C. Avoid techie language
  D. Do not repeat the problem to the customer

EXPLANATION

Don't use techie language or acronyms that the user might not understand.

QUESTION 113

The following is a guideline for good communication with the user:
  A. Check for user errors first
  B. Protect the confidentiality of the data on the PC
  C. Do not repeat the problem to the user
  D. Help the user to understand that solving the problem is the first priority

EXPLANATION

Protect the confidentiality of data on the PC, such as business financial information.

QUESTION 114

The following is true when the customer is involved with solving the problem:
   A. It is acceptable to take over the mouse or keyboard from the user without permission
   B. Do not explain the problem to the customer
   C. Keep the customer informed as you work
   D. Instruct the customer that you need your space to work

EXPLANATION

If the problem is caused by hardware or software, keep the customer informed as you work.

QUESTION 115

The following is true when a customer must make a choice to solve a problem:
   A. Favor the option that makes the most money for the company
   B. Be solution-focused
   C. Be problem-focused
   D. State the options in a way that does not favor any of them

EXPLANATION

When a customer must make a choice, state the options in a way that does not unfairly favor the solution that makes the most money for you as the technician or for your company.

QUESTION 116

Do the following after you have solved a problem:
   A. Verify that the data is fully restored
   B. Instruct the user to file a report about the work done
   C. Avoid filling out your paperwork right away
   D. Close the call before the user asks you for more help

EXPLANATION

If you backed up data before working on the problem and then restored the data from backups, ask the user to verify that the data is fully restored.

QUESTION 117

Do the following after you have solved a problem:
- A. Destroy any backed up data
- B. Close the call before the user asks you for more help
- C. Fill out your paperwork
- D. Instruct the customer to file a report with the problem that you just solved

EXPLANATION

Fill out your paperwork and explain to the customer what you have written.

QUESTION 118

Do not forget to do the following at the beginning of a service call:
- A. Ask for and write down the name and phone number of the caller
- B. Start filling out your paperwork
- C. Tell the customer your hours of service
- D. If your call is accidentally disconnected, wait for the customer to call back

EXPLANATION

Ask for and write down the name and phone number of the caller. Ask for spelling if necessary.

QUESTION 119

The following type of PC support requires more interaction with customers than any other type of PC support:
- A. On-site visit
- B. E-mail support
- C. Internal support
- D. Phone support

EXPLANATION

Phone support requires more interaction with customers than any other type of PC support.

QUESTION 120

If you spend many hours on the phone at a help desk, use the following tool:

A. Wrist-resting pad
B. Headset
C. Ergonomic keyboard
D. Cheap phone

EXPLANATION

If you spend many hours on the phone at a help desk, use a headset. Investing in a high-quality headset will be worth the money.

3

Answer Grid for CompTIA A+ 220-603

Question	Answer	Objective	Question	Answer	Objective
1	A	2.3	36	B	4.1
2	D	2.3	37	D	4.1
3	B	2.3	38	B	4.1
4	C	2.3	39	A	4.1
5	A	2.3	40	C	4.1
6	C	2.3	41	B	4.1
7	B	2.3	42	C	4.1
8	D	2.3	43	D	4.1
9	C	2.1	44	A	4.1
10	D	2.1	45	C	4.1
11	A	2.3	46	A	5.2–5.3
12	B	2.3	47	D	2.1
13	D	2.3	48	B	2.1
14	B	2.3	49	A	5.2–5.3
15	C	2.3	50	B	5.2–5.3
16	A	2.1, 2.3	51	D	2.1
17	B	2.1, 2.3	52	C	5.1–5.3
18	A	2.1, 2.3	53	B	5.1–5.3
19	C	2.1, 2.3	54	C	5.1–5.3
20	D	2.1, 2.3	55	A	2.1, 2.3
21	A	2.1, 2.3	56	D	5.1–5.3
22	D	2.1, 2.3	57	C	5.1–5.3
23	C	2.1, 2.3	58	A	5.1–5.3
24	B	2.1, 2.3	59	D	5.1–5.3
25	A	2.3	60	B	5.2–5.3
26	B	2.3	61	A	5.2–5.3
27	C	2.3	62	B	5.2–5.3
28	D	2.3	63	D	5.2–5.3
29	B	2.1–2.3	64	D	5.2–5.3
30	D	2.1–2.3	65	B	5.4
31	C	2.1–2.3	66	C	5.4
32	A	2.1–2.3	67	A	2.1, 2.3
33	C	4.1	68	D	5.1–5.2
34	D	4.1	69	A	1.3
35	A	4.1	70	C	1.3

Question	Answer	Objective
71	D	1.3
72	B	1.3
73	C	1.3
74	B	1.3
75	D	1.3
76	A	1.3
77	D	1.1
78	C	1.1
79	A	1.2
80	B	1.2
81	C	1.2
82	B	1.2
83	A	1.2
84	D	1.2
85	B	1.2
86	D	1.2
87	A	3.1
88	C	3.1
89	D	3.1
90	C	3.1
91	B	3.1
92	A	3.1
93	C	3.1
94	A	3.2
95	D	3.2
96	B	3.2

Question	Answer	Objective
97	A	3.2
98	B	3.2
99	D	6.1–6.2
100	C	6.1–6.2
101	B	6.1–6.2
102	C	6.1–6.2
103	D	6.1–6.2
104	A	6.1–6.2
105	C	6.1–6.2
106	A	6.1–6.2
107	D	6.1–6.2
108	B	6.1–6.2
109	A	6.1–6.2
110	B	6.1–6.2
111	D	6.1–6.2
112	C	6.1–6.2
113	B	6.1–6.2
114	C	6.1–6.2
115	D	6.1–6.2
116	A	6.1–6.2
117	C	6.1–6.2
118	A	6.1–6.2
119	D	6.1–6.2
120	B	6.1–6.2

3

CompTIA A+ 220-604

QUESTION 1

What is the most popular network architecture used today?

A. Token Ring

B. ATM

C. X.25

D. Ethernet

EXPLANATION

Ethernet (sometimes abbreviated ENET) is the most popular network architecture used today.

QUESTION 2

What is the most popular cabling method for local networks?

A. Coaxial cable

B. Optic-fiber cable

C. Twisted-pair cable

D. Copper wire

EXPLANATION

Twisted-pair cable is the most popular cabling method for local networks.

QUESTION 3

Twisted-pair cable has four pairs of twisted wires for a total of eight wires and uses a connector called:

A. RJ-12

B. RJ-45

C. AUI 15-pin D-shaped

D. ST

EXPLANATION

Twisted-pair cable has four pairs of twisted wires for a total of eight wires and uses a connector called an RJ-45 connector.

QUESTION 4

The following type of cable has a single copper wire down the middle and a braided shield around it:

A. Coaxial cable
B. UTP
C. STP
D. CAT-5

EXPLANATION

Coaxial cable has a single copper wire down the middle and a braided shield around it.

QUESTION 5

The following type of cable transmits signals as pulses of light over glass strands inside protected tubing:

A. Coaxial cable
B. STP cable
C. Fiber-optic cable
D. UTP cable

EXPLANATION

Fiber-optic cables transmit signals as pulses of light over glass strands inside protected tubing.

QUESTION 6

What is the maximum speed of Fast Ethernet?

A. 100 Mbps
B. 150 Mbps
C. 500 Mbps
D. 800 Mbps

EXPLANATION

This improved version of Ethernet (sometimes called 100BaseT) operates at 100 Mbps.

QUESTION 7

What kind of cabling can Gigabit Ethernet use?

A. Thin coaxial cable
B. Single-mode cable
C. STP or UTP rated CAT-3 or higher
D. STP or UTP rated CAT-5 or higher

EXPLANATION

Gigabit Ethernet uses the same cabling and connectors as 100BaseT: STP or UTP cabling rated CAT-5 or higher.

QUESTION 8

The following term refers to the arrangement or shape used to physically connect devices on a network to one another:

A. Sector
B. Topology
C. Segmentation
D. Layout

EXPLANATION

The topology of a network refers to the arrangement or shape used to physically connect devices on a network to one another.

QUESTION 9

The following technology connects each node in a line and has no central connection point:

A. Bus topology
B. Star topology
C. Ring topology
D. Bus–star topology

EXPLANATION

A bus topology connects each node in a line and has no central connection point.

QUESTION 10

The following topology connects all nodes to a centralized hub or switch:

A. Bus topology
B. Star topology
C. Ring topology
D. Bus–ring topology

EXPLANATION

A star topology connects all nodes to a centralized hub or switch.

QUESTION 11

You can think of the following equipment as just a pass-through and distribution point for every device connected to it, without regard for what kind of data is passing through and where the data might be going:

A. Switch
B. Router
C. Border router
D. Hub

EXPLANATION

You can think of a hub as just a pass-through and distribution point for every device connected to it, without regard for what kind of data is passing through and where the data might be going.

QUESTION 12

The following is true about network components:

A. A hub is smarter than a switch
B. A hub is smarter than a router
C. A switch is smarter than a hub
D. A switch is as smart as a hub

EXPLANATION

A switch is smarter and more efficient than a hub and keeps a table of all the devices connected to it.

QUESTION 13

The following is a current wireless technology:

A. Ethernet
B. 802.11
C. FDDI
D. BNC

EXPLANATION

Three current wireless technologies are 802.11 (also called WiFi), WiMAX, and Bluetooth.

QUESTION 14

The following is true about Bluetooth:
  A. Bluetooth transmissions are not encrypted
  B. Bluetooth is a type of Ethernet
  C. Bluetooth transmissions are encrypted
  D. Bluetooth has a range of only 50 meters

EXPLANATION

For security, Bluetooth transmissions are encrypted.

QUESTION 15

The following is true about wireless networks:
  A. Most wireless devices support encryption
  B. Wireless networks do not require their transmissions to be encrypted
  C. Wireless networks do not support encryption
  D. Wireless networks are considered secure

EXPLANATION

Most wireless devices today support one or more standards for encrypted wireless transmission.

QUESTION 16

You can use the following setting to specify that this NIC should connect only to a specific access point:
  A. Mode or network type
  B. Transmission rate
  C. Tx rate
  D. SSID

EXPLANATION

You can enter the name of an access point (SSID) to specify that this NIC should connect only to a specific access point.

QUESTION 17

With WEP encryption, data is encrypted using the following encryption keys:
  A. 12-bit or 24-bit
  B. 24-bit or 32-bit
  C. 64-bit or 128-bit
  D. 128-bit or 256-bit

4

EXPLANATION

With WEP encryption, data is encrypted using either 64-bit or 128-bit encryption keys.

QUESTION 18

The following is true about LCD panels:
  A. Always touch them using a ballpoint pen
  B. LCD panels on notebooks are very resistant
  C. It is acceptable to touch them using sharp objects
  D. Don't touch them with sharp objects

EXPLANATION

LCD panels on notebooks are fragile and can be damaged fairly easily. Take precautions against damaging a notebook's LCD panel. Don't touch it with sharp objects like a ballpoint pen.

QUESTION 19

The following is a good notebook care guideline:
  A. Use an administrator password to protect the system
  B. Pick up or hold the notebook by the display panel
  C. You can move the notebook while the hard drive is being accessed
  D. Put the notebook close to an appliance such as a TV

EXPLANATION

Use an administrator password to protect the system from unauthorized entry, especially if you are connected to a public network.

QUESTION 20

The following is a good notebook care guideline:
  A. You don't need to keep your notebook at a controlled temperature
  B. Keep the lid closed when it is not in use
  C. You don't need to update its OS
  D. It is acceptable to leave the notebook in a dusty or smoke-filled area

EXPLANATION

Keep the lid closed when the notebook is not in use.

QUESTION 21

The following is true about securing a notebook and its data:
  A. When flying, check your notebook as baggage
  B. Leave your notebook in your hotel room
  C. Never use a cable lock to secure your notebook
  D. A notebook is more susceptible to being stolen

EXPLANATION

Because a notebook computer is smaller and lighter than a desktop system and is carried out into public places, it is more susceptible to being stolen.

QUESTION 22

The following is true about notebooks:
  A. Notebooks do not support hibernation
  B. For many computers, pressing the power button or a function key wakes up a system from hibernation
  C. Never use hibernation with a notebook
  D. Desktop PCs do not support hibernation

EXPLANATION

For many computers, pressing the power button or a function key wakes up a system from hibernation.

QUESTION 23

The following equipment provides a means to connect a notebook to a power outlet and provides additional ports to allow a notebook to easily connect to a full-sized monitor, keyboard, and other peripheral devices:
  A. Base station
  B. Docking station
  C. Port replicator
  D. Desktop station

EXPLANATION

A port replicator provides a means to connect a notebook to a power outlet and provides additional ports to allow a notebook to easily connect to a full-sized monitor, keyboard, and other peripheral devices.

QUESTION 24

The following equipment provides the same functions as a port replicator but also adds secondary storage, such as an extra hard drive, a floppy drive, or a DVD drive:

A. Docking station
B. Port base
C. Desktop ports
D. Docking ports

EXPLANATION

A docking station provides the same functions as a port replicator but also adds secondary storage, such as an extra hard drive, a floppy drive, or a DVD drive.

QUESTION 25

To run CMOS setup on a Dell notebook, during booting do the following:

A. Press Esc when the logo appears
B. Press F1 when the logo appears
C. Press F2 when the logo appears
D. Pres Ctrl when the logo appears

EXPLANATION

During booting, press F2 when the logo appears.

QUESTION 26

To run CMOS setup on a Lenovo notebook, during the boot do the following:

A. Press Alt when the logo appears
B. Press F1 when the logo appears
C. Press F2 when the logo appears
D. Press Delete when the logo appears

EXPLANATION

Press F1 when the ThinkPad logo appears during the boot.

QUESTION 27

To run CMOS setup on a Toshiba Libretto notebook, in Windows do the following:

A. Double-click HWSetup in the Control Panel
B. Press F1+Alt
C. Press Esc+Alt+F4
D. Run the Tsetup program

EXPLANATION

In Windows, double-click HWSetup in the Control Panel.

QUESTION 28

The following is important when working inside a notebook case:
   A. Leave the battery pack on the notebook
   B. Do not unplug the AC adapter
   C. Do not remove any PC Card
   D. Unplug the AC adapter

EXPLANATION

It is important to unplug the AC adapter and remove the battery pack before working inside a notebook case.

QUESTION 29

When working inside a notebook case, ground yourself using the following tool:
   A. Antistatic ground strap
   B. Magnetic screwdriver
   C. Paper fingers
   D. Paper mat

EXPLANATION

Ground yourself by using an antistatic ground strap. If no ground strap is available, periodically touch the port to discharge any static electricity on your body.

QUESTION 30

Using regular RAM for video is called:
   A. Video RAMing
   B. Share video
   C. Video sharing
   D. Dynamic video

EXPLANATION

Using regular RAM for video is called video sharing or shared memory.

QUESTION 31

The following is a type of memory used by notebooks:
   A. IDE
   B. SATA
   C. SCSI
   D. Credit card

EXPLANATION

Notebooks use several types of memory, including SO-DIMMs, SO-RIMMs, credit card memory, and proprietary memory modules.

QUESTION 32

The following type of SO-DIMM supports 32-bit data transfers:
   A. 36-pin SO-DIMM
   B. 72-pin SO-DIMM
   C. 100-pin SO-DIMM
   D. 144-pin SO-DIMM

EXPLANATION

72-pin SO-DIMMs support 32-bit data transfers and use FPM or EDO.

QUESTION 33

The following type of notebook memory uses a 64-bit data path and the Rambus technology:
   A. 72-pin SO-DIMM
   B. 100-pin SO-DIMM
   C. 80-pin SO-RIMM
   D. 160-pin SO-RIMM

EXPLANATION

One type of memory for notebooks is the 160-pin SO-RIMM (small outline RIMM), which uses a 64-bit data path and the Rambus technology.

QUESTION 34

The following type of MicroDIMM has 144 pins:
   A. MicroDIMM that contains SDRAM
   B. MicroDIMM that contains DDR SDRAM
   C. MicroDIMM that contains DDR2 SDRAM
   D. MicroDIMM that contains SDRAM2

EXPLANATION

A MicroDIMM that contains SDRAM has 144 pins.

QUESTION 35

The following is true about replacing memory on a notebook:
   A. You always need to remove the keyboard first
   B. It is generally easy to access the memory slots
   C. All notebooks have the memory slots behind the LCD panel
   D. You always need to remove the LCD panel first

EXPLANATION

Most notebooks are designed for easy access to memory.

QUESTION 36

How wide is a notebook hard drive?
   A. 1 inch
   B. 1.5 inches
   C. 2.5 inches
   D. 3.5 inches

EXPLANATION

A notebook hard drive is 2.5 inches wide.

QUESTION 37

You will need the following tool to disassemble a notebook:
   A. Magnetic screwdriver
   B. I/O port
   C. Number 1 Phillips-head screwdriver
   D. Hammer

EXPLANATION

You will need a number 1 Phillips-head screwdriver to disassemble a notebook.

QUESTION 38

The following is true when disassembling a notebook:
   A. As you remove a screw, store or label it
   B. Use a magnetic screwdriver to remove screws
   C. Use a rubber hammer to loosen components and parts
   D. Use a rubber hammer to protect the system against ESD

EXPLANATION

As you remove a screw, store or label it so that you know where it goes when reassembling.

QUESTION 39

The following is true about removing the LCD panel from a notebook:
A. You always need to remove the memory first
B. You always need to remove the keyboard first
C. The LCD panel cannot be removed
D. For many notebooks, you need to remove the keyboard first

EXPLANATION

For many notebooks, to remove the LCD top cover, you must first remove the keyboard.

QUESTION 40

Recently, the industry has turned toward a standard method of connecting an internal card to a notebook using the following specifications:
A. SATA
B. Mini PCI
C. Mini ISA
D. SISA

EXPLANATION

Recently, however, the industry has turned toward a standard method of connecting an internal card to a notebook using the Mini PCI specifications.

QUESTION 41

The following type of Mini PCI card uses a 124-pin stacking connector:
A. Type I
B. Type II
C. Type III
D. Type IV

EXPLANATION

Type III cards use a 124-pin stacking connector.

QUESTION 42

The following component is a card inside the notebook that converts voltage to CPU core voltage:
A. Mini PCI card
B. DC controller
C. Voltage card
D. PCI Voltage

EXPLANATION

The DC controller is a card inside the notebook that converts voltage to CPU core voltage.

QUESTION 43

The following term defines the maximum pages printed per month so as not to void the printer warranty:

A. Warm-up cycle
B. PCL duty
C. PPM cycle
D. Maximum duty cycle

EXPLANATION

The term maximum duty cycle defines the maximum pages printed per month so as not to void the warranty.

QUESTION 44

The following printers work by placing toner on an electrically charged rotating drum and then depositing the toner on paper:

A. Laser printer
B. Ink-jet printer
C. Thermal printer
D. Dye sublimation

EXPLANATION

Laser printers work by placing toner on an electrically charged rotating drum and then depositing the toner on paper as the paper moves through the system at the same speed that the drum is turning.

QUESTION 45

The octagonal mirror in a laser printer is also called:

A. Developing mirror
B. Scanning mirror
C. Fusing mirror
D. Conditioning mirror

EXPLANATION

The octagonal mirror is also called the scanning mirror.

QUESTION 46

The following laser printer component prevents too much toner from sticking to the cylinder surface:

A. Control blade
B. Toner drum
C. Toner cavity
D. Cleaning blade

EXPLANATION

A control blade prevents too much toner from sticking to the cylinder surface.

QUESTION 47

What does Hewlett-Packard call the technology that mixes different colors of ink to produce a new color that then makes a single dot?

A. REt
B. DPI
C. PhotoREt II
D. Ink REt

EXPLANATION

Hewlett-Packard calls this PhotoREt II color technology.

QUESTION 48

The following type of printer uses solid dyes embedded on different transparent films:

A. Laser printer
B. Ink-jet printer
C. Thermal printer
D. Dye-sublimation printer

EXPLANATION

A dye-sublimation printer uses solid dyes embedded on different transparent films.

QUESTION 49

The following type of software can interpret written text so that the text scanned in can be input into a word-processing program:

A. OCR
B. PCL
C. PS
D. PPM

EXPLANATION

Optical character recognition (OCR) software can interpret written text so that the text scanned in can be input into a word-processing program.

QUESTION 50

To install a local printer, you must log onto a Windows 2000/XP system using the following account:

A. Printer
B. Install
C. Support
D. Administrator

EXPLANATION

To install a local printer, log onto the system as an administrator.

QUESTION 51

To share a local printer using Windows, you must install the following component:

A. Client for Microsoft Networks
B. Printer Sharing for Microsoft Networks
C. File and Printer Sharing
D. Printer Client

EXPLANATION

To share a local printer using Windows, you must install File and Printer Sharing.

QUESTION 52

In Windows 98, you can choose to associate the network printer with a printer port to satisfy a DOS application using the following tool:

A. Add MS-DOS Printer
B. Capture Printer Port
C. Capture MS-DOS Printer
D. Add MS-DOS Port

EXPLANATION

You can choose to associate the network printer with a printer port such as LPT1 to satisfy the DOS application. Click Capture Printer Port, and then select the port from the drop-down menu in the Capture Printer Port dialog box.

QUESTION 53

The following is true about network printers:
  A. They have Windows 3.1 installed
  B. They have Linux installed
  C. They have no OS installed
  D. They have UNIX installed

EXPLANATION

Because a network printer has no OS installed, the printer's NIC contains all the firmware needed to communicate over the network.

QUESTION 54

Normally, when Windows receives a print job from an application, it places the job in a queue and prints from the queue. This process is called:
  A. Spooling
  B. Stacking
  C. Sorting
  D. GDI

EXPLANATION

Normally, when Windows receives a print job from an application, it places the job in a queue and prints from the queue. This process is called spooling.

QUESTION 55

The following is true when replacing an ink cartridge on an ink-jet printer:
  A. You must turn the printer off before replacing the cartridge
  B. You must turn the printer on to replace the cartridge
  C. You must unplug the printer's power cord
  D. You must replace the black ink cartridge every time you replace a color cartridge

EXPLANATION

To replace a cartridge, turn on the printer and open the front cover.

QUESTION 56

Manufacturers of high-end printers provide the following kits, which include specific printer components, step-by-step instructions for performing maintenance, and any special tools or equipment you need to do maintenance:
  A. Spooling
  B. Cartridge maintenance
  C. Re-inking
  D. Printer maintenance

EXPLANATION

Manufacturers of high-end printers provide printer maintenance kits, which include specific printer components, step-by-step instructions for performing maintenance, and any special tools or equipment you need to do maintenance.

QUESTION 57

The maintenance plan for the HP Color LaserJet 4600 printer says the black ink cartridge should last for about:

A. 6,000 pages
B. 9,000 pages
C. 11,000 pages
D. 13,000 pages

EXPLANATION

The maintenance plan for the HP Color LaserJet 4600 printer says the black ink cartridge should last for about 9,000 pages.

QUESTION 58

The following tool is made of nylon fibers that are charged with static electricity and easily attract the toner like a magnet:

A. Antistatic vacuum cleaner
B. Toner-certified vacuum cleaner
C. Extension magnet brush
D. Toner strap

EXPLANATION

The long-handled extension magnet brush is made of nylon fibers that are charged with static electricity and easily attract the toner like a magnet.

QUESTION 59

The following is true when cleaning an ink-jet printer:

A. You cannot clean the ink-jet nozzles
B. You must change the ink-jet nozzles every time you clean the printer's drum
C. You must clean the transfer roller using a wet cloth
D. For some models, you can use software to clean the ink-jet nozzles

EXPLANATION

For some ink-jet printers, you can use software to clean the ink-jet nozzles or align the cartridges, which can help improve print quality.

QUESTION 60

You can manually clean an ink cartridge nozzle using a cotton swab dipped in the following type of water:

   A. Distilled
   B. Tap
   C. Cold
   D. Hot

EXPLANATION

Dip a cotton swab in distilled water (not tap water) and squeeze out any excess water.

QUESTION 61

To install a scanner in a Windows 2000/XP system, you must log on as:

   A. Printing user
   B. Technician
   C. Administrator
   D. Installer

EXPLANATION

To install a scanner, log on to the Windows 2000/XP system as an administrator.

QUESTION 62

For flat-bed scanners, you can clean the glass window using the following:

   A. Mild glass cleaner
   B. Acetone
   C. Isopropyl alcohol
   D. Cotton swab dipped in tap water

EXPLANATION

For flat-bed scanners, you can clean the glass window with a soft dry cloth or use mild glass cleaner.

QUESTION 63

The following is true when cleaning a scanner's device to scan negatives and slides:

   A. Use abrasive glass cleaner
   B. Don't use any type of glass cleaner
   C. Use acetone
   D. Use a soft dry cloth

EXPLANATION

You can clean this surface with a soft dry cloth or use mild glass cleaner.

QUESTION 64

When troubleshooting a printer, to eliminate the printer as the problem, first check that the printer is on, and then:
  A. Check the network cable
  B. Print a test page
  C. Press the menu button
  D. Check the power cable

EXPLANATION

To eliminate the printer as the problem, first check that the printer is on, and then print a test page.

QUESTION 65

If you suspect that the printer cable is bad, you can use the following tool to check it:
  A. Multimeter
  B. Transfer roller
  C. Fuse tester
  D. Printer strap

EXPLANATION

If you suspect that the cable is bad, you can use a multimeter to check it.

QUESTION 66

Parallel cables longer than the following can sometimes cause problems with printing:
  A. 1 feet
  B. 2 feet
  C. 5 feet
  D. 10 feet

EXPLANATION

Parallel cables longer than 10 feet can sometimes cause problems.

QUESTION 67

An ECP parallel port requires the use of the following type of channel:
  A. PCA
  B. DMA
  C. DPI
  D. PCI

EXPLANATION

An ECP parallel port requires the use of a DMA channel.

QUESTION 68

You can delete all print jobs in the printer's queue using the following Windows 2000/XP tool:

    A. Printers window

    B. Device Manager

    C. Printer and Faxes window

    D. Applications menu

EXPLANATION

You can delete all print jobs in the printer's queue using the Windows 2000/XP Printer and Faxes window.

QUESTION 69

The following is true about PC toolkits:

    A. All kits contain only essential tools

    B. All kits contain only non–essential tools

    C. All toolkits come with an antistatic vacuum cleaner

    D. Most PC toolkits contain items you really can do without

EXPLANATION

Most PC toolkits contain items you really can do without.

QUESTION 70

The following is true about PC support tools:

    A. They should not include a ground bracelet

    B. Keep your tools in a toolbox designated for PC troubleshooting

    C. They should not include a Torx screwdriver

    D. Your tools should not include tweezers

EXPLANATION

Keep your tools in a toolbox designated for PC troubleshooting.

QUESTION 71

The following statement is true:

A. You cannot recover a computer using a hidden recovery partition on its hard drive

B. You can use a loop-back plug to recover and reinstall Windows

C. Some computers have a hidden recovery partition in their hard drives

D. You cannot recover Windows XP Home Edition from the recovery partition on the hard drive

EXPLANATION

For some brand-name computers, the hard drive contains a hidden recovery partition that you can use to reinstall Windows.

QUESTION 72

The following is true about cleaning solutions:

A. Most of them contain flammable and poisonous material

B. All PC cleaning solutions are free of flammable material

C. All PC cleaning solutions are free of poisonous material

D. All PC cleaning solutions are safe for your skin

EXPLANATION

Most of these cleaning solutions contain flammable and poisonous materials. Take care when using them that they don't get on your skin or in your eyes.

QUESTION 73

To find out what to do if you accidentally become exposed to a dangerous solution, check out the following:

A. CRTS

B. MSDS

C. DSMS

D. VDSS

EXPLANATION

To find out what to do if you accidentally become exposed to a dangerous solution, look on the instructions printed on the can or check out the MSDS.

QUESTION 74

If you have a problem that prevents the PC from booting and that you suspect is related to hardware, you can install the following tool in an expansion slot on the motherboard and then attempt to boot:

   A. POST diagnostic card
   B. Torx LED card
   C. MSDS diagnostic card
   D. BIOS diagnostic LED

EXPLANATION

You can install a POST diagnostic card in an expansion slot on the motherboard and then attempt to boot.

QUESTION 75

The following is a good tip to protect your equipment:

   A. Smoking around your computer will not affect it
   B. Do not use a firewall
   C. Don't move or jar your computer when it's turned on
   D. You can ignore using antivirus software

EXPLANATION

Don't move or jar your computer when it's turned on. Before you move the computer case even a foot or so, power it down.

QUESTION 76

The following is true when physically protecting your computer:

   A. High humidity cannot affect your computer
   B. For optimum airflow, leave empty expansion slots and bays uncovered
   C. Leave the PC turned off for weeks or months
   D. Install dehumidifiers in places with high humidity

EXPLANATION

High humidity can be dangerous for hard drives.

QUESTION 77

The following is true when protecting storage media:

   A. Keep floppy disks and hard drives away from magnetic fields
   B. Open the shuttle window on a floppy disk to clean inside
   C. Expose them to direct sunlight
   D. Expose them to extreme cold

EXPLANATION

Keep floppy disks and hard drives away from magnetic fields.

QUESTION 78

The following is true about a PC preventive maintenance plan:
- A. It is a waste of time
- B. Any organization is better without one
- C. If your company has no established plan, do not create one
- D. It tends to evolve from a history or pattern of malfunctions within an organization

EXPLANATION

A preventive maintenance plan tends to evolve from a history or pattern of malfunctions within an organization.

QUESTION 79

The following is true when creating a preventive maintenance plan:
- A. Dusty environments can mean less maintenance
- B. Clean environments can mean more maintenance
- C. Dusty environments can mean more maintenance
- D. Clean environments mean no maintenance at all

EXPLANATION

Dusty environments can mean more maintenance, whereas a clean environment can mean less maintenance.

QUESTION 80

How often should you ensure that chips and expansion cards are firmly seated?
- A. Monthly
- B. Yearly
- C. Every two years
- D. Every five years

EXPLANATION

You should ensure that chips and expansion cards are firmly seated once a year.

QUESTION 81

How often should you clean the floppy drive?

A. Weekly
B. Monthly
C. Yearly
D. When the drive does not work

EXPLANATION

Clean the floppy drive only when the drive does not work.

QUESTION 82

How often should you defragment the hard drive and scan the drive for errors?

A. Weekly
B. Monthly
C. Every four months
D. Yearly

EXPLANATION

You should defragment the drive and scan the drive for errors once a month.

QUESTION 83

The following is true about maintaining a printer:

A. Never replace an ozone filter
B. Do not use printers that use ozone filters
C. Do not re-ink ribbons
D. It is safe to use recharged toner cartridges

EXPLANATION

Don't re-ink ribbons or use recharged toner cartridges.

QUESTION 84

How often should you replace a printer's ozone filter?

A. As recommended by the manufacturer
B. Yearly
C. Every two years
D. Every five years

EXPLANATION

If the printer uses an ozone filter, replace it as recommended by the manufacturer.

QUESTION 85

The following is an important part of preventive maintenance:
   A. Re-inking your printer's ribbon
   B. Ridding the PC of dust
   C. Recharging your printer's toner cartridge
   D. Leaving your PC's empty bays open

EXPLANATION

Ridding the PC of dust is an important part of preventive maintenance.

QUESTION 86

The following is true when dealing with dust on a PC:
   A. A regular vacuum might produce ESD
   B. It is safe to use a regular vacuum inside a PC case
   C. Never use compressed air to blow the dust out of the chassis
   D. Never use compressed air to blow the dust out of the power supply

EXPLANATION

Some PC technicians don't like to use a vacuum inside a PC because they're concerned that the vacuum might produce ESD.

QUESTION 87

How should you dispose of chemical solvents and cans?
   A. Bury them
   B. Smash them
   C. Check for local laws and regulations
   D. Burn them

EXPLANATION

Check with local county or environmental officials for laws and regulations in your area for proper disposal of these items.

QUESTION 88

The following is a good tip to protect components against static electricity:
   A. Keep them close to your clothes
   B. Always use a magnetic screwdriver
   C. Use a graphite pencil to change DIP switch settings
   D. Keep components away from your hair and clothing

EXPLANATION

To protect against static electricity, keep components away from your hair and clothing.

QUESTION 89

The following is true when working inside a computer case:
  A. A charge of only 10 volts can damage electronic components
  B. A charge of 10 volts cannot damage electronic components
  C. A charge of 6,000 volts cannot damage electronic components
  D. A charge of 8,000 volts cannot damage electronic components

EXPLANATION

A charge of only 10 volts can damage electronic components.

QUESTION 90

How many volts can a monitor discharge onto the screen?
  A. Less than 10 volts
  B. No more than 1,500 volts
  C. At most 5,000 volts
  D. As much as 29,000 volts

EXPLANATION

A monitor can discharge as much as 29,000 volts onto the screen.

QUESTION 91

The following is true when working inside a laser printer:
  A. You must wear a ground bracelet
  B. You must be grounded
  C. You do not want to be grounded
  D. Laser printers do not store electricity in capacitors

EXPLANATION

When working inside a monitor, laser printer, or power supply, you don't want to be grounded, because you would provide a conduit for the voltage to discharge through your body.

QUESTION 92

The following is a process that allows the CPU to receive a single instruction and then execute it on multiple pieces of data:
  A. MMX
  B. SIMD
  C. SSE2
  D. SSE3

EXPLANATION

SIMD, which stands for "single instruction, multiple data," is a process that allows the CPU to receive a single instruction and then execute it on multiple pieces of data rather than receiving the same instruction each time each piece of data is received.

QUESTION 93

The following Intel technologies help with repetitive looping, which happens a lot when the CPU is managing audio and graphics data:

A. PowerNow! and 3DNow!

B. 3DNow! and HyperTransfer!

C. HyperTransfer! and PowerNow!

D. MMX and SSE

EXPLANATION

MMX and SSE help with repetitive looping, which happens a lot when the CPU is managing audio and graphics data.

QUESTION 94

The following is a processor instruction set designed by AMD to improve performance with 3D graphics and other multimedia data:

A. MMX

B. 3DNow!

C. SSE

D. PowerNow!

EXPLANATION

For its processors, AMD uses 3DNow!, a processor instruction set designed to improve performance with 3D graphics and other multimedia data.

QUESTION 95

The following is a technology used by AMD to increase processor bandwidth:

A. 3DNow!

B. SIMD

C. HyperTransport!

D. PowerNow!

EXPLANATION

AMD uses HyperTransport! to increase bandwidth.

QUESTION 96

The following is a technology used by AMD to improve processor performance and lower power requirements:
A. PowerNow!
B. 3DNow!
C. HyperTransport!
D. SSE3

EXPLANATION

AMD uses PowerNow! to improve a processor's performance and lower power requirements.

QUESTION 97

The following computer component can record sound, save it in a file on your hard drive, and play it back:
A. Video card
B. Sound card
C. Game card
D. Joystick card

EXPLANATION

A sound card can record sound, save it in a file on your hard drive, and play it back.

QUESTION 98

How many separate channels of sound information are supported by the Surround Sound standard?
A. 8
B. 10
C. 12
D. 16

EXPLANATION

The Surround Sound standard supports up to eight separate sound channels of sound information.

QUESTION 99

The following is true about a digital sound channel:
A. It cannot support subwoofer speakers
B. It is affected by background noise
C. It does not have background noise
D. It is not supported by the Surround Sound standard

EXPLANATION

There is no background noise on the channel.

QUESTION 100

The following is generally considered the standard for PC sound cards:

A. RCA
B. 3DNow!
C. S/PDIF
D. Sound Blaster

EXPLANATION

Sound Blaster is generally considered the standard for PC sound cards.

QUESTION 101

The following term defines the number of samples taken of the analog signal over a period of time:

A. Sampling rate
B. Surround sound
C. Digital sound
D. SIMD

EXPLANATION

The sampling rate of a sound card is the number of samples taken of the analog signal over a period of time.

QUESTION 102

What is the file system used by CDs?

A. NTFS
B. EFS
C. FAT
D. CDFS

EXPLANATION

CD (compact disc) drives use the CDFS (Compact Disc File System).

QUESTION 103

What is the file system used by DVDs?

A. FAT
B. CDFS
C. UDF
D. NTFS

EXPLANATION

DVD drives use the newer UDF file system.

QUESTION 104

The following term refers to raised areas or bumps on the surface of a CD:

A. Pits

B. Lands

C. Tracks

D. Sectors

EXPLANATION

The surface of a CD stores data as pits and lands. Lands are raised areas or bumps.

QUESTION 105

The following term refers to recessed areas on the surface of a CD:

A. Lands

B. Tracks

C. Sectors

D. Pits

EXPLANATION

Pits are recessed areas on the surface of a CD.

QUESTION 106

The process of imprinting a plastic CD with lands and pits is called:

A. Hitting the CD

B. Burning the CD

C. Heating the CD

D. Fixing the CD

EXPLANATION

During manufacturing, the plastic CD is imprinted with lands and pits. (The process is called burning the CD.)

QUESTION 107

The effect of using a constant speed as the CD disc turns is called:

A. SIMD

B. CDFS

C. CLV

D. CAV

EXPLANATION

The effect of constant speed as the disc turns is called constant linear velocity (CLV).

QUESTION 108

The following term means that data was written to the CD at different times:
   A. Multisessions
   B. Single session
   C. CLV sessions
   D. CAV sessions

EXPLANATION

To say a disc was created in multisessions means that data was written to the disc at different times rather than in a single long session.

QUESTION 109

With the following technology, the CD rotates at a constant speed, just as is done with hard drives:
   A. CLV
   B. CAV
   C. Multisessions
   D. Single session

EXPLANATION

With CAV, the disc rotates at a constant speed, just as is done with hard drives.

QUESTION 110

The following term describes a CD drive that can only read a CD and not write to it:
   A. CD-ROM
   B. CD-RW
   C. CD-R
   D. CAV-ROM

EXPLANATION

If a CD drive can only read a CD and not write to it, the drive is called a CD-ROM drive.

QUESTION 111

The following type of CD drive can burn either a CD-R or CD-RW disc:
A. CD-R
B. CD-CAV
C. CD-RW
D. CD-ROM

EXPLANATION

A CD-RW drive can burn either a CD-R or CD-RW disc.

QUESTION 112

A parallel ATA interface is also called:
A. SATA
B. SCSI
C. PCI-P
D. EIDE

EXPLANATION

A parallel ATA interface is also called EIDE.

QUESTION 113

What is currently the most popular interface for an optical drive?
A. EIDE
B. SCSI
C. PCI
D. SATA

EXPLANATION

Currently, the most popular interface for an optical drive is parallel ATA, also called EIDE.

QUESTION 114

For ATA/100 hard drives and above, use the following type of cable:
A. 25-conductor IDE
B. 30-conductor IDE
C. 40-conductor IDE
D. 80-conductor IDE

EXPLANATION

For ATA/100 hard drives and above, you use an 80-conductor IDE cable.

QUESTION 115

The following term describes a DVD that is recordable in two layers:
   A. DVD-ROM
   B. DVD-R
   C. DVD-R (DL)
   D. DVD-RW

EXPLANATION

DVD-R (DL) describes a DVD that is recordable in two layers.

QUESTION 116

The following is true about DVD or CD drives:
   A. DVD drives can work properly even if they are standing vertically
   B. DVD drives will not work properly if they are standing vertically
   C. CD drives can work properly if they are standing vertically
   D. DVD drives must always be standing vertically

EXPLANATION

A CD or DVD drive will not properly read a CD or DVD when the drive is standing vertically.

QUESTION 117

The following statement is true about a computer:
   A. The hardware is always the most valuable component
   B. The software is always the most valuable component
   C. The monitor is the most valuable component
   D. In many cases, the most valuable component is the data

EXPLANATION

In many cases, the most valuable component on the desktop is not the hardware or the software, but the data.

QUESTION 118

What are the current capacities of backup tapes?
   A. 10 to 400 GB compressed
   B. 20 to 800 GB compressed
   C. 30 to 900 GB compressed
   D. 40 to 900 GB compressed

EXPLANATION

Tapes currently have capacities of 20 to 800 GB compressed.

QUESTION 119

The following is true about tape drives:
   A. Older tape drives require less cleaning than newer tape drives
   B. Newer tape drives do not need cleaning
   C. Newer tape drives need less cleaning than older tape drives
   D. Older tape drives do not need cleaning

EXPLANATION

Newer tape drives don't need cleaning as often as the older ones did.

QUESTION 120

The following equipment retensions, vacuums, inspects, and wipes tapes automatically:
   A. Magnetic tape cleaner
   B. Tape-ROM
   C. Tape-RW
   D. Tape+R

EXPLANATION

A magnetic tape cleaning machine retensions, vacuums, inspects, and wipes tapes automatically.

ANSWER GRID FOR COMPTIA A+ 220-604

Question	Answer	Objective	Question	Answer	Objective
1	D	2.1	36	C	2.1
2	C	2.1	37	C	1.2
3	B	2.1	38	A	1.2
4	A	2.1	39	D	1.2
5	C	2.1	40	B	2.1, 2.3
6	A	2.1	41	C	2.1, 2.3
7	D	2.1	42	B	2.1, 2.3
8	B	2.1	43	D	3.1
9	A	2.1	44	A	3.1
10	B	2.1	45	B	3.1
11	D	2.1	46	A	3.1
12	C	2.1	47	C	3.1
13	B	4.2	48	D	3.1
14	C	4.1–4.2	49	A	3.1
15	A	4.2	50	D	3.2
16	D	4.2	51	C	3.2
17	C	4.1–4.2	52	B	3.2
18	D	1.2–1.3	53	C	3.2
19	A	1.2–1.3	54	A	3.2
20	B	1.2–1.3	55	B	1.2
21	D	4.1–4.2	56	D	3.3–3.4
22	B	1.3	57	B	3.3–3.4
23	C	2.1–2.2	58	C	3.3–3.4
24	A	2.1–2.2	59	D	3.3–3.4
25	C	1.2	60	A	3.3–3.4
26	B	1.2	61	C	3.2–3.4
27	A	1.2	62	A	3.2–3.4
28	D	1.2	63	D	3.3–3.4
29	A	1.2	64	B	3.3–3.4
30	C	2.1–2.2	65	A	3.3–3.4
31	D	2.1–2.2	66	D	3.3–3.4
32	B	2.1–2.2	67	B	1.2
33	D	2.1–2.2	68	C	3.3–3.4
34	A	2.1–2.2	69	D	1.2
35	B	2.1	70	B	1.2

4

Question	Answer	Objective
71	C	1.2
72	A	5.1
73	B	5.1
74	A	1.2
75	C	5.1
76	D	5.1
77	A	1.2
78	D	1.3
79	C	1.3
80	B	1.3
81	D	1.3
82	B	1.3
83	C	5.1
84	A	5.1
85	B	1.3
86	A	5.1
87	C	5.1
88	D	5.1
89	A	5.1
90	D	5.1
91	C	5.1
92	B	1.1
93	D	1.1
94	B	1.1
95	C	1.1

Question	Answer	Objective
96	A	1.1
97	B	1.1
98	A	1.1
99	C	1.1
100	D	1.1
101	A	1.1
102	D	1.1
103	C	1.1
104	B	1.1
105	D	1.1
106	B	1.1
107	C	1.1
108	A	1.1
109	B	1.1
110	A	1.1
111	C	1.1
112	D	1.1
113	A	1.1
114	D	1.1
115	C	1.1
116	B	1.1–1.3
117	D	1.1
118	B	1.1
119	C	1.1–1.3
120	A	1.1–1.3

Index

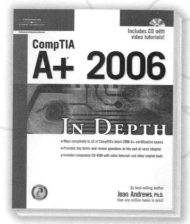
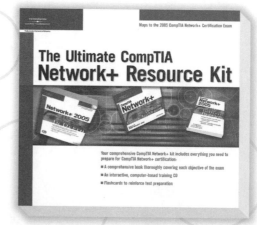